Tomie de Paola in the Classroom

Written by Sharon Rybak

Illustrated by Gary Mohrmann

Cover by Gary Mohrmann

Copyright © 1993, Good Apple

Good Apple, Inc.
299 Jefferson Road
P.O. Box 480
Parsippany, NJ 07054-0480

SIMON & SCHUSTER *A Paramount Communications Company*

Copyright © 1993, Good Apple

ISBN No. 0-86653-719-8

Printing No. 987654

Good Apple
1204 Buchanan St., Box 299
Carthage, IL 62321-0299

Dedication

This book is dedicated to Tomie de Paola who has given me years of joyful resources for teaching children. "Grazie"

I would also like to acknowledge my partner teacher Michelle Patton. As a first-year teacher she has shared her outstanding ideas and helped to contribute to this book.

Finally, to Jerry Aten—Thank you.

iii

GA1436

Table of Contents

GA1438

Introduction

This book is designed to help teachers use the books of Tomie de Paola in a whole language classroom. Tomie's books are rich with extension possibilities. Many of the books tie in naturally with units in science, social studies, math and other curriculum areas.

The selection of books being used in this book are not the complete library of Tomie de Paola's books. This very versatile author has a wide variety of books that can enrich any primary classroom. The books selected have the most variety and lead to the most workable extension activities.

Each of the books has a number of activities that blend with the theme. Each book includes some type of skill and comprehension activity, writing, higher level thinking skills, extension activities, and product production.

Each book also has a lead page with suggested activities for the teacher. Bulletin board suggestions, discussion questions, class projects, arts and crafts, and other valuable extensions have been included.

A profile of the author and some resources to discover more about this American treasure, Tomie de Paola, are also included.

Finally, book cover designs for each book are included at the end of the book. These can be used for student writing or extension activities.

GA1436

About Tomie de Paola

Tomie de Paola's name is pronounced TOM-ee de-POW-la. He was born in Connecticut in 1934. He currently lives in a renovated farmhouse in New Hampshire. Children can see the inside of his beautiful home in *Country Home Magazine*, June 1985.

The children will quickly gain a sense of the author through the reading of *The Art Lesson*. Tomie always wanted to be an artist and did draw pictures on his sheets while he held a flashlight.

After graduating from high school, Tomie attended Pratt Institute where he studied art for four years. After college he started working as an illustrator for books that were written by other people. The first book he illustrated was called *Sound* and the first book he wrote and illustrated was called *The Wonderful Dragon of Timlin* which was published in 1966.

Tomie de Paola is not married and has no children, but he does have some wonderful Abyssinian cats named Foshay and Dayton and an Ocicat named Bomba.

During his free time he enjoys cooking, cross-country skiing, biking, walking, reading and watching movies. He enjoys popcorn and even has his own popcorn machine on wheels.

Christmas is his favorite season. The New Hampshire farmhouse is decorated with hundreds of candles, and four Christmas trees are adorned with 3000 lights. He once enjoyed an early Christmas in August and held the entire celebration and lighting of trees just for fun.

There is no doubt to anyone who reads his books that the spirit of the child is alive and well inside Tomie de Paola. He has been able to touch children with his love of family in books like *Now One Foot, Now the Other* and his sense of fun in books such as *Bill and Pete*. Many of the books are instructional such as *The Popcorn Book* and "*Charlie Needs a Cloak*."

The diversity of the work and the consistency of the illustrations make the books of Tomie de Paola favorites of children. The children can quickly identify the artistic style and are eager to become involved in the stories which are always different and engaging.

GA1436

The Art Lesson

Reading *The Art Lesson* to the class is a good way to introduce the unit about Tomie de Paola. This is a wonderful story of Tomie's quest to be a real artist. He has artists in the family who encourage his talents and tell him not to copy. All of his grandparents admire his work and proudly display his masterpieces. Tomie cannot wait to go to school where he will get real art instruction.

His kindergarten experience is disappointing. The paint is so thin it cracks right off the paper, and the art teacher doesn't teach the class until first grade. Tomie's brother reminds him that in first grade you get only one sheet of paper.

Finally, first grade arrives and Tomie is filled with anticipation the night before the first art lesson. Unfortunately, the first grade teacher is not pleased with Tomie and the sixty-four crayons he received for his birthday. The end of this story is poignant and offers teachers and students something to think about in the pursuit of learning.

Crayons

No symbol is more representative of children's art than the crayon. *The Art Lesson* offers many activities related to the wonderful crayon.

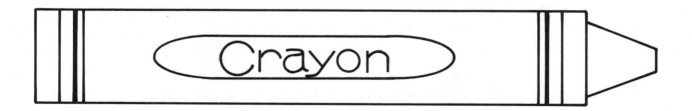

Bulletin Board Idea
Make a large crayon box with the name Crayon on the front. The children can fill the box with large construction paper crayons. The children can write about their favorite stories, draw pictures of their favorite books or tell what they like about Tomie de Paola books.

GA1436

The Quick-sand Book	Michael Bird-Boy	Oliver Button Is a Sissy	The Kids' Cat Book	Pancakes for Breakfast	The Art Lesson	Old Mother Hubbard and Her Dog
The Legend of the Blue-bonnet	Chicken Feet in Your Soup	The Knight and the Dragon	Old Befana	Hey, Diddle, Diddle	Strega Nona	Mary Had a Little Lamb
Andy	Bill and Pete	"Charlie Needs a Cloak"	Merry Christmas, Strega Nona	Fin M'Coul	Helga's Dowry	Strega Nona's Magic Lessons

Crayons

Tomie ♡ de Paola

Strega Nona

Strega Nona

The story *Strega Nona* is a delightful lesson in following directions and being responsible. Engaging the children in conversation about these topics can lead to many enlightening discussions in a classroom. Another topic is temptation. Big Anthony did not resist the temptation to do what he was told not to do. Have your children discuss or write about times when they did or did not give in to temptation.

Anthony wanted to show the townspeople that he was important and for a brief time he was a hero. Discuss with the children the problem with doing things in order to show off to your friends.

This book also leads to some interesting discussions about punishment. When Strega Nona says "the punishment must fit the crime" what does that mean? Share different things children do wrong and think of punishments that might fit the crimes, such as taking cookies from the cookie jar or fighting with a sister or brother.

Here is a list of other possible activities.
- Teach everyone a magic trick.
- Find out about all the different kinds of pasta and make a pasta picture.
- Dye pasta using a small amount of alcohol and food coloring. Use the pasta for craft projects.
- Discuss the chores your children have. How much do they think Big Anthony should be paid by today's wages?
- Discuss barricades and when they are used today. Have the children make a barricade that will stop a stone falling down a slanted board created in the classroom.
- Have a spaghetti meal in your classroom. Try to eat by winding the spaghetti around a fork.
- Create a tune for Strega Nona's little song.
- Make a storefront display as Big Anthony tries to get rid of the excess pasta.
- Write a newspaper article after the pasta event and tell what happened. Use headlines, dates and times when writing the story.

GA1436

Strega Nona

1. **Before You Read**–Strega Nona is a grandma witch with a magic touch. Draw a picture of your grandma or favorite aunt and tell about something *magic* she can do.

What is her name? _____

What can she do? _____

_____

_____

_____

_____

_____

2. Look at the pictures and try to guess when and where this story takes place.

When: _____

Where: _____

3. Who is this book dedicated to? _____

_____

_____

5   GA1436

4. Strega Nona helped people with their problems. Make up your own magic *potion* that will fix a broken heart.

Ingredients: _____

_____

_____

_____

_____

_____

5. We can't see the sign Strega Nona put on the town square. What did it say?

GA1436

6. Do you remember what a verb is? Define. _____

_____

7. Do you remember what a noun is? Define. _____

_____

8. In this activity you are to match the verb with the noun and write it in a phrase. These are all the jobs of poor Big Anthony.

Verbs	Write your answer with the verb first and the noun second. (Pick the flower.)	Nouns
pick		house
wash		dishes
milk		garden
sweep		vegetables
weed		goat
fetch		water
	Make up one of your own.	

9. Anthony got paid three coins and two other things. What were they?

a. _____

b. _____

GA1436

10. What do you think *grazie* means?_____

_____

11. What do you think *si* means?_____

_____

12. Let's change Strega Nona's little song. Can you make up the second
    and fourth lines and make them rhyme?

    Bubble, bubble pasta *pan*
    Boil me some pasta_____
    I'm hungry and it's time to *munch*
    Boil enough pasta _____

13. Strega Nona blew three kisses. Make up other things that she could
    have done three times.

Draw	Draw	Draw
Tell	Tell	Tell
_____	_____	_____
_____	_____	_____
_____	_____	_____
_____	_____	_____
_____	_____	_____
_____	_____	_____
_____	_____	_____
_____	_____	_____
_____	_____	_____
_____	_____	_____

14. Have you ever told the truth when you were not believed? What happened? _____

_____

_____

_____

_____

_____

How did you feel? _____

_____

_____

_____

15. Big Anthony was a hero. In your own words tell what you think a hero is. _____

_____

_____

_____

16. Who are your heroes? _____

_____

_____

_____

17. The town was covered with pasta. Think of three silly uses for extra pasta.

a. _____

b. _____

c. _____

GA1436

18. Look at Tomie de Paola's drawings. He draws characters with simple shapes and dark black lines. Inside the shapes he shades and colors.

Try to use this style in a picture of your own.

GA1436

19. The townspeople made a barricade. In your own words tell what a barricade does._____

_____

_____

_____

_____

20. Think of three other punishments for Big Anthony.

a. _____

b. _____

c. _____

21. What was your favorite part of this book? Why?_____

_____

_____

_____

_____

_____

_____

_____

GA1436

Story Plot Sequence for *Strega Nona*

Strega Nona blew three kisses the last time.

Directions:
1. Read all ten boxes.

2. Cut out the boxes.

3. Paste them in the correct order on the next page as they happened in the story.

Strega Nona puts a sign on the square.

Help Needed

Strega Nona blew three kisses the first time.

Big Anthony eats all the pasta.

Strega Nona leaves to visit Strega Amelia.

Big Anthony sings "Bubble, Bubble Pasta Pot."

The townspeople built a barricade.

The pasta pot overflows over the town.

Big Anthony brags to the townspeople.

Strega Nona gets rid of warts.

GA1436

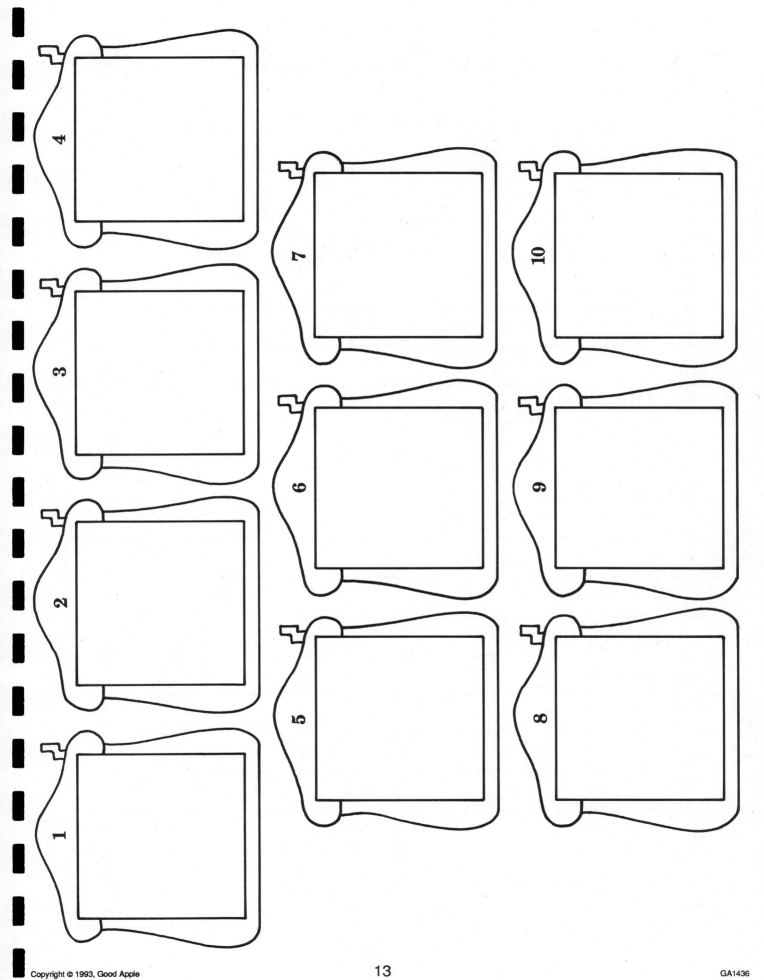

13

GA1436

Strega Nona **Crossword Puzzle**

Across
1. means "Grandma Witch"
3. Strega Nona's helper
5. *yes* in Italian
6. Strega Nona cooked in this.
7. The pot kept _____.

Down
2. *thank you* in Italian
4. what Big Anthony didn't see
8. The story took place in this town.
9. Strega Nona had the _____ touch.
10. This was Big Anthony's punishment.

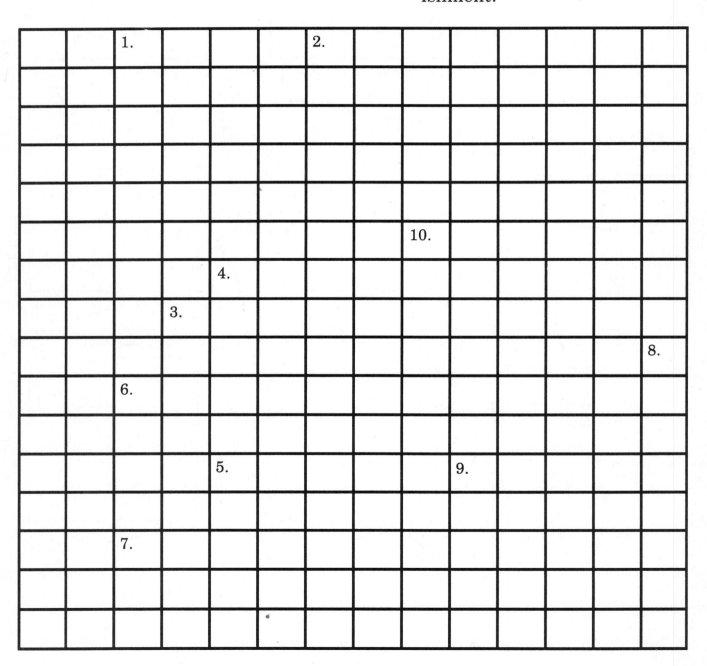

GA1436

Strega Nona Pasta

Here's what's cooking.
Ingredients:

Steps you need to follow to make the perfect pasta.

First, _____
_____
_____
_____
_____
_____
_____
_____
_____
_____

GA1436

Village Times

Accident Nearly Causes Disaster

_____
_____
_____
_____
_____

Strega Nona Says . . .

_____
_____
_____
_____
_____
_____

Picture from the scene of the pasta spill.

Job Wanted: _____
_____
_____
_____
_____
_____ Big Anthony

For Sale—Cheap!

_____
_____
_____
_____
_____
_____

GA1436

The Popcorn Book

17

The Popcorn Book

The Popcorn Book is certainly one book you can enjoy on all levels. The book is filled with popcorn facts and fantasy. Children love eating the finished product and everyone learns a greater appreciation for that special little seed.

Using the popcorn for extended math activities is a valuable learning experience and one that can easily be developed in the classroom. Popcorn can be measured, counted and of course used in an exciting lesson on volume.

If you look through catalogs or if you are fortunate enough to have a store or a cornfield near your home, try to find an ear of popcorn still on the cob. We had a taste test in our classroom and the ear of popcorn beat every leading brand of popcorn with overwhelming votes.

One way to make the popcorn from a cob is to remove it from the cob and cook it as you normally would. But, another fun method is to stick the ear of corn in a brown paper bag and put it in a microwave oven for a few minutes. Your children will be amazed to see a bag filled with popcorn.

If you use the book in the winter, leave the popcorn out until it is stale and then string it with cranberries for the birds. The children use large dull-tipped needles.

Popcorn is also good for measurement. We used a large tub and filled it with popcorn. The children were able to use tablespoons, cups, quarts, half gallons and gallons in their measurement comparisons.

We then tried to estimate the amount of space needed for thirty pieces of popcorn popped and unpopped. This lesson on volume is quite graphic and dramatic for children.

Finally, don't forget to eat lots of popcorn. I found it easiest to bring a popcorn popper into the class so we could have popcorn whenever we wanted. Serving up popcorn can easily be done by putting it into a coffee filter. It's a good size, inexpensive and reusable for a few servings.

Read *How Much Is a Million?* by Steven Kellogg.

GA1436

The Popcorn Book
by
Tomie de Paola

Name: _____

Before you read, write a list of all the things you already know about popcorn.

_____ _____

_____ _____

_____ _____

_____ _____

_____ _____

Turn to the first page where you first see the two little boys. What can you tell by looking at the picture?

_____

_____

_____

_____

_____

What are the boys' names? _____ and _____

19

Popcorn Facts

1. How much older was the corn found in New Mexico than the popcorn found in Peru?

_____

_____

_____

3. What did Columbus see in San Salvador?

_____

_____

_____

_____

_____

2. How old was the popcorn found in the bat cave in New Mexico?

_____

4. Find Peru on a map. What continent is it on and what color is it on your map?

_____

_____

_____

5. What did they do with the popcorn they found in Peru?

_____

_____

7. Name three types of corn.

a. _____

b. _____

c. _____

6. By looking at the picture, what are two things you can tell about Peru?

a. _____

b. _____

8. How old were the kernels found in Peru?

_____

GA1436

Indians Cooking Their Popcorn

Popcorn on a Stick

How They Did It	What Was the Problem?	Picture
_____	_____	
_____	_____	
_____	_____	
_____	_____	
_____	_____	

Throw the Kernels into the Fire

How They Did It	What Was the Problem?	Picture
_____	_____	
_____	_____	
_____	_____	
_____	_____	
_____	_____	

Popcorn in Clay Pots

How They Did It	What Was the Problem?	Picture
_____	_____	
_____	_____	
_____	_____	
_____	_____	
_____	_____	

21

Popcorn Soup and Other Delicious Recipes

The Iroquois people liked popcorn soup. And the colonists liked popcorn for breakfast cereal. Now it's your turn to come up with a creative recipe using popcorn.

Name of your popcorn recipe: _____

Ingredients: (things that go into your recipe) Don't forget to include how much you will need of each item, such as cups, tablespoons, teaspoons and number (for example, four eggs).

_____   _____

_____   _____

_____   _____

_____   _____

_____   _____

_____   _____

Steps to Making Your Recipe

1st _____

2nd _____

3rd _____

4th _____

5th _____

How long do you cook your recipe? _____

At what temperature do you cook it? _____

How many people will it serve? _____

GA1436

Make your own cereal box cover for popcorn cereal.

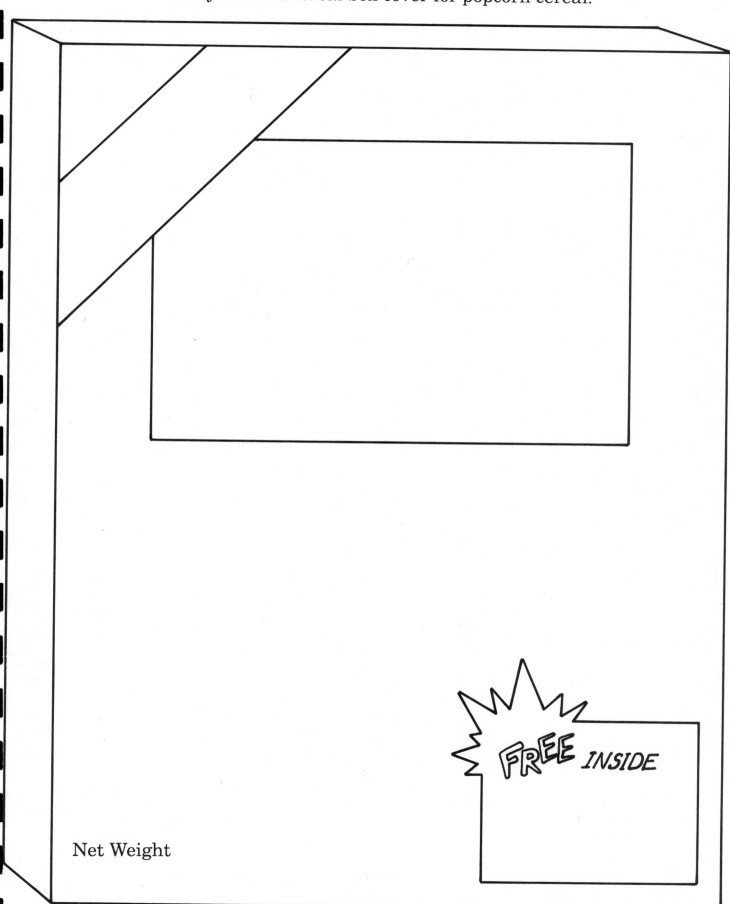

Net Weight

FREE INSIDE

23

GA1436

Popcorn Eaters of America

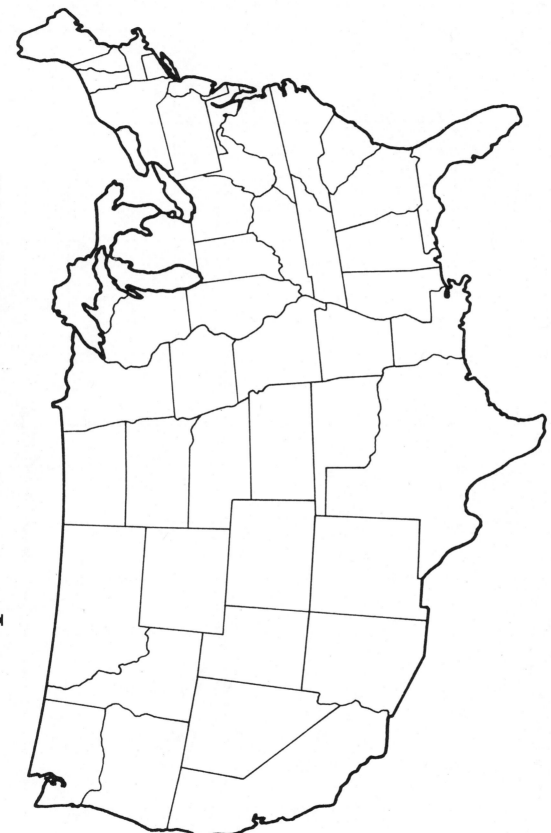

1. Look at a large map of the United States.
2. Find Milwaukee on the big map and color a red circle in the spot for that city.
3. Find Minneapolis on a big map and color a green circle in the spot for that city.
4. Find Chicago on a big map and color a blue circle in the spot for that city.
5. Color the Midwest on your map yellow.
6. Find Seattle on a big map and color a purple circle in the spot for that city.

24

500,000,000 Pounds of Popcorn!
(That's 500 Million Pounds)

Color the pieces of popcorn on the graph so it will show how much popcorn is eaten in movies, circuses, ball games, and county fairs. How much of it is kept for seed and sold to other countries and how much of it is eaten at home.

	Popcorn Eaten at Movies, Ball Games, Circuses, County Fairs	Popcorn Sold to Other Countries and Kept for Seed	Popcorn Popped at Home
100%			
90%			
80%			
70%			
60%			
50%			
40%			
30%			
20%			
10%			
0%			

GA1436

Facts and Opinions About Popcorn

Read the statement about popcorn and then tell if it is fact or opinion. Remember a fact is something that is true or can be proven true, and an opinion is what someone thinks or feels.

1. _____ Popcorn is best when it is stored in a jar so the kernels keep their moisture.

2. _____ Popcorn tastes very good with butter and salt.

3. _____ Kernels left in the bottom of a pan are called "old maids."

4. _____ Popcorn pops because the moisture on the inside of the kernel heats up and pops open the shell.

5. _____ A little demon lives inside a popcorn kernel.

6. _____ The smallest type of popcorn is called strawberry.

7. _____ Eating black popcorn is better than yellow popcorn.

8. _____ Popcorn is the best snack in the world.

9. _____ Salt in the pan before the kernels are popped will make the popcorn tough.

10. _____ Popcorn is very nice to eat.

GA1436

Popping with Popcorn Activities

Writing Activities

• Use adjectives to describe a piece of popcorn as it cooks and pops and words to describe how it tastes and sounds when it is eaten.

• Try to imagine that you are the first Indian to put a piece of popcorn in the fire. How did it happen? What did you think? How did it taste?

• Pretend you are Tony and Tiny's mother, and leave the boys directions on how to make popcorn.

• Make up your own silly popcorn story.

Step Book to Popcorn Making

| Fold down at 2" (5.08 cm). | Fold down at 3" (7.62 cm). | Fold down at 4" (10.16 cm). | Fold down at 5" (12.7 cm). |

Steps for Making Popcorn
1.
2.
3.
4.
5.
6.
7.

Use four pieces of 8½" x 11" (21.6 x 27.94 cm) paper. Fold the first piece down by 2" (5.08 cm); fold the second piece down by 3" (7.62 cm); fold the third piece down by 4" (10.16 cm); and fold the fourth piece down by 5" (12.7 cm).

Nest the pieces of paper together and staple them at the top.

Now you are ready to write and illustrate the steps to making popcorn.

GA1436

Popcorn Evolution

Today I eat my popcorn;
It is easy as can be.
Microwave is the new age;
It's ready one, two, three.

My dad made popcorn on the stove
With oil and salt and butter.
Just three kernels to start out.
They'd pop with such a flutter.

My grandma cooked her popcorn
Upon an open hearth
In a basket, black with soot,
The popcorn burnt and dark.

When Grandma cooked her popcorn
Her nose and cheeks so red,
She ate her popcorn just like me
Before she went to bed.

Sharon Rybak

GA1436

Michael Bird-Boy

GA1436

Michael Bird-Boy

The book *Michael Bird-Boy* allows children a simple look at the effects of pollution. It also offers an opportunity for many fun and educational learning experiences.

The activities allow the children to do some comparing and contrasting, vocabulary and productive thinking. Another activity can be a cooking lesson. This recipe is done on a per child basis. It will need to be cooked in a conventional oven.

Honey Yum Apples
Each child will need
- 1 apple
- 1 tablespoon (15 ml) of honey
- 1 tablespoon (15 ml) of orange juice
- 2 marshmallows (8 miniature)
- 1 table knife
- 1 tart tin

Have each child cut the apple into small pieces, place the pieces in the tart tin, and put his name on the tin with magic marker. Cover the apples with the honey and orange juice and cut up marshmallows. Bake at 375° F (191° C) for 30 minutes or until soft. Top with a marshmallow while still warm.

Invite a beekeeper into your classroom for a visit, or buy some honey with the honeycomb inside. Your children might also enjoy a honey tasting contest using various types of honey.

Finally, give the children time to act out the story or the steps to making honey using the bees, hive and flower art project. Children love being the one with the hive on their head and the bees swarming around. Each bee must touch a flower before it can return to the hive. Fewer flowers make a good lesson on supply and demand when each bee cannot find a flower.

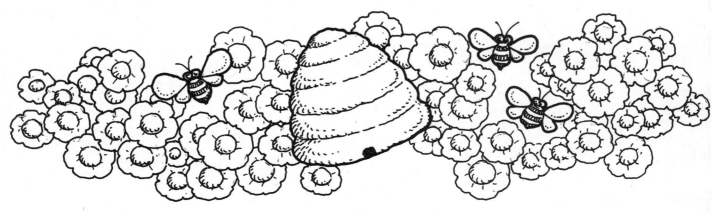

GA1436

Michael Bird-Boy, Wake Up!

These are the things Michael Bird-Boy did in the morning.		These are the things that you do in the morning.	
1st	2nd	1st	2nd
3rd	4th	3rd	4th

How are the things you and Michael Bird-Boy do the same? _____

_____

_____

How are the things you and Michael Bird-Boy do different? _____

_____

_____

GA1436

Michael Bird-Boy Does His Chores

These are the jobs that Michael Bird-Boy does.	These are the jobs that you do.
1.	1.
2.	2.
3.	3.
4.	4.
5.	5.
6.	6.

How are Michael's jobs the same as your jobs? _____

_____

_____

How are Michael's jobs different from your jobs? _____

_____

_____

GA1436

Spring, Summer, Fall, Winter

Michael Bird-Boy enjoyed the weather and the seasons because each day and season was different. Draw something from each season and then write the name of the season under the picture.

GA1436

Mix and Match

Boss-Lady was making Genuine Shoo-Fly Artificial Honey Syrup in her factory. See if you can match each of the words in the project name to its meaning.

1. genuine _____

2. shoo _____

3. fly _____

4. artificial _____

5. honey _____

6. syrup _____

a. yell to chase away

b. made by man, not nature

c. made by bees, sweet

d. a thick, sweet, sticky liquid

e. a small insect

f. not artificial or fake

7. Can you tell which two words mean the opposite?

_____   _____

When you shoo the fly what do you do?

_____

GA1436

Bees to Honey

Bees go back to the hive.

Flowers grow.

Bees go to the flower and drink nectar.

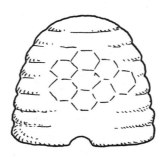

Bees make honeycombs from beeswax.

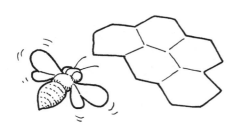

The bees turn nectar into honey and put it into the honeycombs.

Boss-Lady's factory produces the honey.

Color each box.
Cut out each box.
Put the boxes in order.

GA1436

Create a label for the old Genuine Shoo-Fly Artificial Honey Syrup.

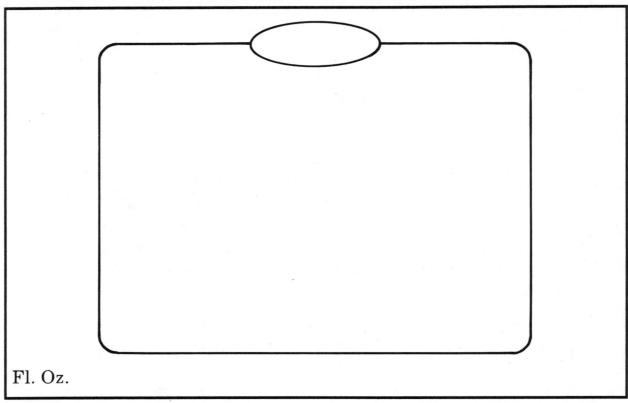

Fl. Oz.

Create a label for the new honey project.

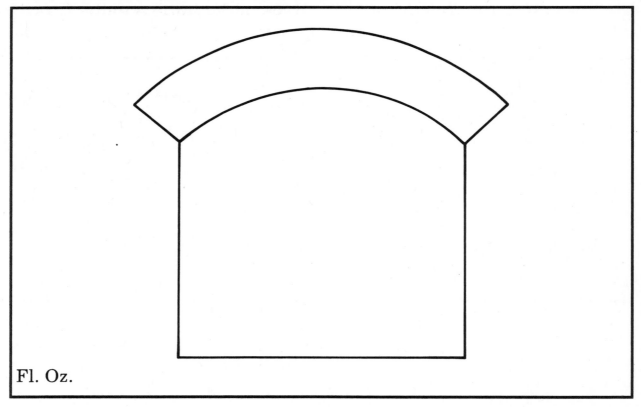

Fl. Oz.

GA143

A Honey of a Party

Write an invitation to Michael Bird-Boy's party with Boss-Lady.

Please come to my party.

We are going to celebrate _____

_____

Date: _____

Time: _____

Place: _____

R.S.V.P.

Please don't forget the _____.

GA1436

Bees–Hives–Flowers

Materials:

egg carton cups (cardboard)
yellow paint
white construction paper
small black pom-poms
black and green pipe cleaners
a yellow ski hat for the hive
small cupcake liners for the flower centers

Paint the egg carton cups bright yellow and set aside to dry. Use craft glue to attach a black puff for the head and a small pipe cleaner for the stinger. Use markers to make the stripes and attach the wings. When they are complete, let the children attach some to a yellow hat that will be the hive.

GA1436

AU / LCCC
Teacher Educational Resource Center
1005 North Abbe Road
CC008
Elyria, Ohio 44035
(440) 366-4082

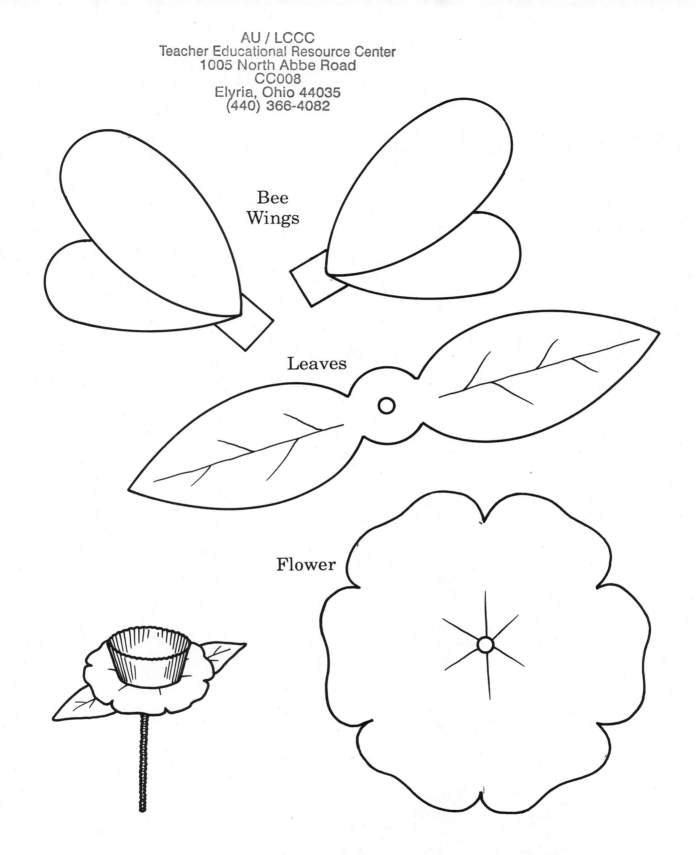

Bee
Wings

Leaves

Flower

Color and cut out the flower shape. Stick a green pipe cleaner through the center of the flower and attach a small cupcake liner. Stick the green pipe cleaner through the center of the leaves and pull up to the flower.

GA1436

The Bees . . . . Love Me

The bees are buzzing
Around my head,
But they want flowers
And pollen instead.

I try to tell them
My flower is fake,
But they keep making
The same mistake.

See over there, those
Flowers are real.
I don't like having
So much bee appeal!

Sharon Rybak

GA1436

Fin M'Coul

The Giant of Knockmany Hill

41

GA1436

Fin M'Coul

The vocabulary in this book is rich. The children will enjoy the clever way Oonagh was able to trick Cucullin with her magic. The legend of Fin M'Coul is quite old. Before you begin let me give you some background on the legend of Fin M'Coul.

Finn Mac Cool is the spelling sometimes used for the Irish hero. The characters often have battles with strange and supernatural beings. The stories are set in the Southern region of Ireland and many originate in the countryside of Killarney. These stories are of a folklore and fairy tale nature. The stories contain many magic charms and little fairies. It is common for the stories to have loose ends and elements that don't make sense. They can contain elements of strange occurrence and sheer fantasy.

GA1436

Here is a lead story you can share with your children on the birth and young life of Finn Mac Cool.

The Young Life of Finn Mac Cool

Many years ago there lived a man called Cool MacTrenmor. This man was the great captain of the clan Bascna of Leinster. Now this captain of the clan named Cool was in a battle near the town today called Dublin. One of Cool's warriors wounded a man named Aed in the eye during the battle and from that day forward the man whose eye was injured was called Goll which means "one eye."

The fighting continued for many days and in the end Goll's men killed Cool as revenge for the lost eye of Goll. After Cool was killed, Goll's men took a treasure bag from Cool filled with the secrets of the clan.

News of Cool's death soon reached his wife, who was ready to give birth to their child. With great sadness she fled into the wilderness with two trusted women. In the woods, Cool's widow gave birth to a boy-child. The mother, fearing for her child's safety, fled the woods leaving the child to be raised by the two women.

The boy grew into a strong child who was trained in the ways of the wild woods. He could hunt and bring down a bird from the sky with a fling of his stone. He could chase deer on his bare feet and could hunt the badger, fox and falcon.

One day, during his travels through the woods, he came upon a clan where the boys of his age were playing hurley. This game was played with a broad netless stick and a ball. They told him the rules, and he quickly beat the best of the players. The next day he returned and half of the boys played against just him, and he beat the lot. In the evening the boys told their clan chief about the strength of the boy whose name they did not know. "He was strong and tall and had the hair as bright as barley when it whitens in the sun." "If he is fair," said the chief, "then there is only one name for him and that is Finn." From that day forward he was known as Finn.

The chief talked of the strange child to a friend who told another friend, and soon everyone was talking of the boy with great strength and skill. The talk soon came to Goll, and the description of the boy ran fear through Goll who knew that the boy could be the lost and only son of Cool whose mother had disappeared. Goll smelled danger. Goll told his men to go and find this boy named Finn.

GA1436

One of Finn's mothers was a wise woman who could see the future in the water cupped in her hand. She told the other woman and together they spoke to Finn.

"You are being hunted, and you must leave. Goll and his men will try to kill you since you are the man who should be chief of your clan. Go quickly and leave the glen."

Finn took only his spear, his sling and his warmest cloak. As Finn traveled he gathered a group of other young men who, like him, were young and fierce and daring. Together these young men traveled into Leinster to find the old followers of his father's Clan of Bascna. As the young men climbed the hills, they came into a glen with a small house. From the house dressed in rags came men with tattered clothes and grey hair. They were carrying simple weapons and were thinking they were meeting the enemy. Young Finn stepped forward and identified himself as the son of Cool, and with that the men cried out with great loud voices. They opened a bag that had been taken from his father at his death that held the treasure of the clan. "We have been waiting for you to come to take back the rightful place as clan chief," said the men.

Finn told the men to hold the treasure bag until he called for it. Then he left and went to do the last of the things needed to be done before he could lead.

Finn went to study poetry and learn the history and ancient wisdom of his people. He went to live with Finegas who was waiting to catch the Salmon Fish of Knowledge from the dark river. For seven years Finegas had been trying to catch this fish and eat it so he could become the keeper of the knowledge. As soon as Finn arrived, Finegas caught the fish.

Finegas now wanted Finn to cook the fish, but he did not want Finn to eat even a bite of the fish because in doing so he would get the knowledge. Finegas told Finn to cook the fish, which he did. When he returned to serve the Salmon Fish of Knowledge, Finn had a different look on his face, and Finegas could see the difference. "You have eaten my fish!" screamed Finegas."No," said Finn, "I simply put my thumb in my mouth because of a burn I received." "The damage is done; eat the fish," screamed Finegas. "The juice from the fish has entered your body and now you are the keeper of the knowledge." From that day forward Finn would only need to put his thumb to his lips, and he had the power to see the future and the meanings of all mystery. He could also heal by giving someone a drink of water from his cupped hand.

GA1436

Fin M'Coul

1. Who is the main character and what is his wife's name?

   _____

   _____

2. How do you think his hometown got the name Knockmany Hill?

   _____

   _____

3. Fin was working with his kin on the causeway. What do you think *kin* and *causeway* mean?

   kin: _____

   causeway: _____

4. Cucullin was very strong. Two things in the story tell us how strong he really was. What are they?

   a. _____

   b. _____

5. Why was it important to Cucullin to beat Fin M'Coul?

   _____

   _____

6. When Oonagh heard that Cucullin was after Fin, she tried to sooth him. What five things did she do to make Fin more comfortable?

   a. _____

   b. _____

   c. _____

   d. _____

   e. _____

Braiding the Magic Woolen
Threads of Oonagh

In the story Oonagh works a charm that is taught to her by the fairies.
She starts with nine woolen threads, each a different color.

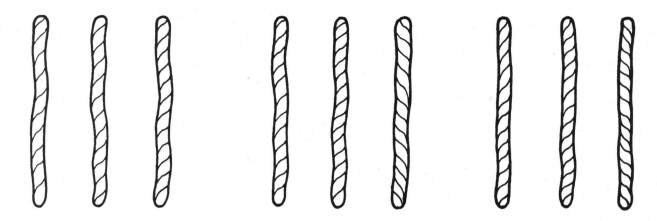

Red   Yellow   Orange   Green   White   Black   Purple   Pink   Blue

Then she braids them together to make three rings. Follow the braids
and color them correctly.

7. Then Oonagh put the braids in three places. Where were they?

a. _____

b. _____

c. _____

Now it's your turn to make a magic braid. Take three different colors of
yarn and learn to braid. Tie your braid around your wrist and make a
magic wish.

GA1436

Could So! Could Not!

Oonagh did some magical things to convince Cucullin that Fin was too much a giant to fight. Some of the things in the story could have happened in real life, and some of the things could not have happened. Listed below are some of the things that happened. Check if it COULD or COULD NOT HAVE HAPPENED and then tell WHY.

	This COULD have happened.	This COULD NOT have happened.	Tell why you gave your answer.
1. Oonagh braids the wool.			_____ _____ _____
2. Oonagh bakes 21 loaves of bread with frying pans.			_____ _____ _____
3. Cucullin thinks that Fin is a baby.			_____ _____ _____
4. Cucullin has a thunderbolt in his pocket.			_____ _____ _____
5. Fin eats the cheese and Cucullin eats the stones.			_____ _____ _____
6. Fin and Oonagh sit down to tea.			_____ _____ _____

GA1436

Modern Day Giants

Look through magazines or draw a picture of two people that look like Fin M'Coul and Cucullin. Tell why you chose these two pictures.

Fin M'Coul	Cucullin

How did Cucullin lose his magic?

_____

_____

_____

_____

_____

_____

_____

Draw a picture showing where all of Cucullin's magic lies.

48

GA1436

Fin M'Coul Fairies

In the story *Fin M'Coul*, Fin and his wife Oonagh lived among the fairies. Make your own fairies using clothespins, construction paper and small bits of cloth.

49

GA1436

Leprechauns–Giants–Fairies

The story *Fin M'Coul* says that the land was filled with leprechauns, giants and fairies. These are all imaginary creatures so we can have our own ideas about what they looked like, where they lived, what they liked to do, how they dressed and what they liked to eat.

Leprechauns

What does your leprechaun look like? Draw a picture.

What does your leprechaun like to do for fun?

_____

_____

_____

_____

_____

Where does your leprechaun live? Draw and tell.

_____

_____

_____

_____

_____

GA1436

 # Giants

What does your giant look like?	Where does your giant live? Draw a picture.
	What does your giant eat? _____ _____ _____ _____ _____ _____
	What does your giant do for fun? _____ _____ _____ _____ _____ _____

GA1436

 # Fairies

What does your fairy look like? Draw a picture.	What special magic does your fairy have?
	_____ _____ _____ _____ _____ _____ _____ _____

Where does your fairy sleep at night? Draw a picture.	What is a fairy's favorite food? Draw and tell.
	  _____ _____ _____

GA1436

The Knight and the Dragon

53

GA1436

The Knight and the Dragon

This book lends itself to some delightful writing experiences. The children can create dialogue for the characters and can be encouraged to use quotation marks. Children may enjoy acting out the story using puppets or props.

Extend upon the concept of silent letters using the book vocabulary such as *knight*, *fought*, *castle*, *fighting*, *through* and *fight*. A letter from the knight and the dragon encourages the children to identify the words with silent letters and to use them in a letter.

The theme of the library and the helpful librarian is also a good theme to extend upon. The children can alphabetize the books, and they can create their own little books that teach how to fight a dragon and how to fight knights.

During discussion with the class be sure to take note of the following questions:

1. Who helped the knight and the dragon solve their problem and how was it done?
2. How did the knight use his suit of armor after he decided not to fight?
3. What do the *K* and *D* stand for on the restaurant sign?
4. What jobs did the knight and dragon do at their restaurant?
5. What other kind of company could the knight and the dragon have started other than a restaurant?

Bulletin Board Idea

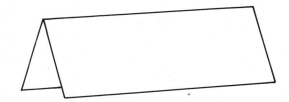

Step 1: Fold it the "hot dog" way.

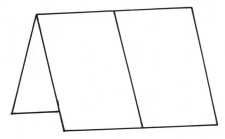

Step 2: Open it up and fold it the "hamburger" way.

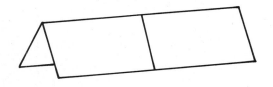

Step 3: Fold it in half again.

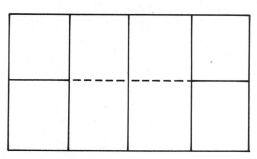

Step 4: Open it up and cut on the dotted line.

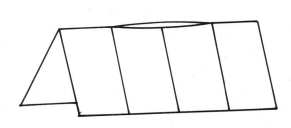

Step 5: Open your paper and fold it the "hot dog" way again.

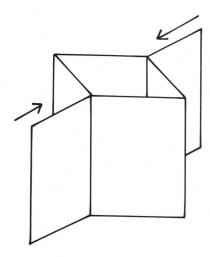

Step 6: Push the two ends together to create the book.

55

GA1436

Title:

How to Make Armor

The End

How to Make Weapons

What to Watch Out for When Fighting

What to Do if You Don't Win the Fight

How to Practice

How to Write Letters to Dragons

GA1436

Title:

How to Swish Your Tail

How to Look Fierce

The End

What to Watch Out for When Fighting

What to Do if You Don't Win the Fight

How to Practice

How to Write Letters to Knights

GA1436

Be the Castle Librarian

The knight has made a mess of the library, and the librarian has too much work to do! Help her put the library books back in ABC order. Cut and paste.

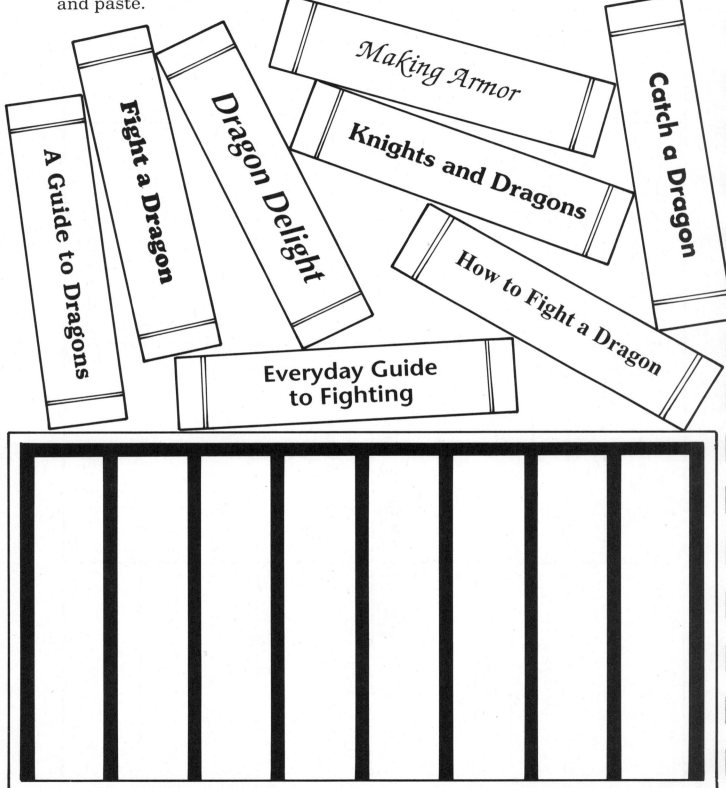

Making Armor

Fight a Dragon

Dragon Delight

Knights and Dragons

Catch a Dragon

A Guide to Dragons

How to Fight a Dragon

Everyday Guide to Fighting

My Diary as a Knight

Write in the knight's diary and tell what happened.

One day I was in my castle . . . _____

_____

_____

_____

I went to the castle library . . . _____

_____

_____

_____

I made a fire . . . _____

_____

_____

_____

I worked on my weapons . . . _____

_____

_____

_____

I practiced by . . . _____

_____

_____

Then I sent a letter . . . _____

_____

_____

The dragon and I fought . . . _____

_____

_____

But in the end . . . _____

_____

_____

GA1436

My Diary as a Dragon

Write in the dragon's diary and tell what happened.

One day I was in my cave . . . _____

_____

_____

_____

I rummaged through . . . _____

_____

_____

I practiced . . . _____

_____

_____

Then I practiced . . . _____

_____

_____

I went outside and tried to . . . _____

_____

_____

Then I sent a letter . . . _____

_____

_____

The knight and I fought . . . _____

_____

_____

But in the end . . . _____

_____

_____

GA14

The Secret Silent Words of the Knight and the Dragon

Read the letter from the dragon to the knight. See if you can find all the secret silent words in the letter. Circle the words with silent letters. When you are done write a letter back to the dragon pretending that you are the knight. Use the secret silent words in your letter so the dragon will know the letter is from the knight.

Dear Knight,

Do you want to fight? I am rough and tough, and you can't catch me! Once I almost got caught by another knight, but I fought him and got away. I will go through the woods and meet you at the castle. I like fighting, don't you? See you soon.

The world's toughest dragon,

Dragon

What Happened After the Knight and the Dragon Opened the Bar-B-Q?

Try to imagine what life was like for the knight and the dragon. Did they have problems? What kinds of problems would come from a knight and a dragon working together?

Tell your own story about the knight and the dragon; then illustrate each part of the story and tell what happened.

1.	2.
3.	4.
5.	6.

GA14

Watch Out for the Chicken Feet in Your Soup

Watch Out for the Chicken Feet in Your Soup

This book lends itself to lots of classroom cooking experiences. In my classroom I have made both chicken soup and bread from scratch. It really is easier than you would think. Below are some recipes with classroom adaptations and explanations for making some exciting cooking magic in the classroom.

Making Bread

The trick to making wonderful bread is the temperature of the water you use to dissolve the yeast. The yeast is a one-celled organism that needs three things in order to activate. The first is heat, the second air and the third is food, which in the yeast's case is some sort of sugar. The air and the sugar are not difficult, but starting with warm water and keeping the dough warm is the real trick. If you remember you are dealing with an organism, you will make great bread.

The recipe on the next page is my favorite bread recipe. I usually make two batches at the same time. This allows more participation and one usually turns out different than the other for comparison's sake. The children take turns doing the measuring and the mixing, and I try to give every child an opportunity to knead the dough. If they wash and flour their hands, the job is really not that messy.

To bake the dough I use a toaster oven and a mini muffin tin. Not every muffin tin fits in every toaster oven, so check it out in advance. We spray some oil in the mini muffin tin and roll the dough into balls. We can cook twelve little muffins in a few short minutes. This makes for lots of samples and a quick cooking time. It is done in the classroom, and the children thoroughly enjoy the process.

Remember to keep everyone safely away from the toaster. Don't forget your pot holders and spray oil to keep the bread from sticking.

While the bread is baking you might as well have the children make homemade butter. Buy heavy whipping cream at the grocery store and, if possible, use clear jars for the children to share the cream. If the children are using glass, then have them sit on a carpeted area and pass the jar carefully. As the cream is shaken, the heavy parts of fat begin to stick together. When it is done, the butter will be in a large glob and the liquid will be skim milk. You will need to add some salt to the mixture since most children are not familiar with the taste of sweet butter.

64

Bread Recipe

1 package active dry yeast
$1\frac{1}{2}$ cups (360 ml) warm water (about 110° F [43.3° C])
1 tablespoon (15 ml) honey
5 cups (1200 ml) all purpose flour

As you can see, this recipe is easy because of the limited number of ingredients. Begin by carefully measuring the temperature of the water. Use a thermometer if you have one. If not, the water should be hot to the touch but not so hot that it would scald or burn your fingers. If the water is too hot, it will kill the yeast organism.

Add the honey once the yeast is dissolved. Then begin to add the flour a cup at a time. The only way to mix the dough is with your hands, so let the children dig in the bowl with their clean hands and get the job done.

Let the children continue to mix and knead the dough until it is smooth. Add flour if necessary to keep it from sticking, but don't add too much or the dough will be tough.

Line some cookie sheets with wax paper and let the children roll the dough into balls. If the balls touch, they will rise into each other so try to keep them apart. After all the balls have been rolled, cover them with wax paper and then cover them with some of the children's coats, just like in the story! It keeps the bread nice and warm and draft free while it rises.

In twenty to thirty minutes uncover the dough and begin to bake. Keep the unbaked dough under the coats to keep it warm until baking time.

I usually have the oven at about 400° F (204° C), and the little bread balls bake in less than ten minutes. If you want to get fancy, you can brush the tops of the balls with melted butter or milk before baking. This will nicely brown them.

GA1436

Additional Classroom Activities for *Watch Out for the Chicken Feet in Your Soup*

Clay Bread Dolls
The children enjoy making the bread dolls that Joey's grandmother made for the boys. Use modeling clay or bread dough clay for the children to play with in their free time.

Spelling Words in Your Soup
Make a large bowl of soup, and put it on the bulletin board. Don't forget the chicken feet sticking out of the soup. Have this week's spelling words or story vocabulary float in the soup, and put some alphabet noodles in a center for the children to practice their spelling.

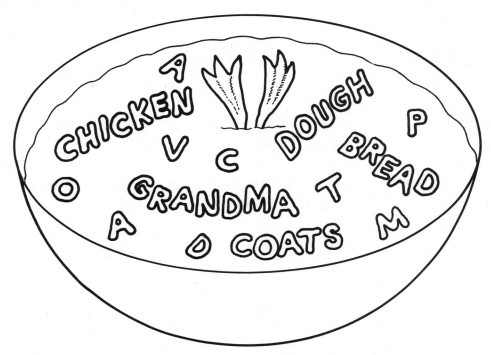

Read *Chicken Soup with Rice* by Maurice Sendak.

The Italian words used in the story have the following English translations:

bambino–child or baby
ragazzi–boys
caro–dears (an affectionate term)
zuppa–soup
arreviderce–good-bye

A Visit to Grandma's House

On the first page of the book *Watch Out for the Chicken Feet in Your Soup*, Joey and Eugene are walking to Grandma's house. Joey tells Eugene that his grandma is nice, BUT she pinches his cheeks, has lots of funny old stuff, is always cooking and she talks funny.

In the columns below list the different ways that Joey's grandma talks funny, different things she cooks and look for all the different things around Grandma's house.

Different Words	Things She Cooks	Things in Her House

Tell about your own grandma and the funny things she has at her house, things she says and special things she cooks.

_____

_____

_____

_____

_____

GA1436

Joey and Eugene

As Joey and Eugene visit Grandma, they each have different feelings. Tell about each boy's feelings as they go through the story. You must read and look at the pictures to get the answers, and you must think about feelings.

Before Eugene and Joey get to Grandma's house,

Joey feels _____

Eugene feels _____

When Joey and Eugene get to Grandma's house and Grandma puts the coats on her bread,

Joey feels _____

Eugene feels _____

When the boys sit down to eat soup,

Joey feels _____

Eugene feels _____

When the boys sit down to eat spaghetti,

Joey feels _____

Eugene feels _____

When Grandma makes bread dolls,

Joey feels _____

Eugene feels _____

When the boys leave to go home,

Joey feels _____

Eugene feels _____

GA1436

Bill and Pete

Bill and Pete
Go down the Nile

GA1436

Background Information About Ancient Egypt

Children will need some background information to completely enjoy the Bill and Pete books. Since the stories take place in Egypt, it is important to share some information with your children.

Find Egypt on a world map with the children and identify the Nile River. The Nile is the most important geographical element when understanding this corner of the world. Away from the Nile River the land is a desert which is called the Red Land. Over 90 percent of Egypt is covered with desert. The land that is rich and fertile for the Egyptians is the land that surrounds the Nile and the canals that extended from the Nile. One of the reasons the land is so rich is that the Nile River floods every year. When it floods, swelling waters carry rich deposits of silt which then provide fertile land for the farmers' crops.

The water also allows for movement on boats. This provided the ancient Egyptians a means to travel and visit other regional areas. The Nile was rich with fish and hippopotami. The hippo was considered an evil omen and in reality could cause trouble for the fishermen by capsizing their boats.

The time of ancient Egypt that was ruled by the pharaohs was after 3000 B.C. The word *pharaoh* means "great house." A pharaoh was considered to be powerful and to be a god in the Egyptian community. The Queen was also considered to be a goddess. It was because of this belief that such elaborate burial sites were created for these god-humans.

The Egyptians believed that you could live forever if you were given the proper burial. Kings were buried with food, weapons, boats, gold, and hundreds of items that would take them to the afterlife. The rituals of burial are the elements found in the Bill and Pete stories.

Mummies: The bodies were wrapped in cloth that was laced with jewels and oils. The body might take weeks to prepare. The Egyptians believed that a person's Ka, which is the body's double, could bring it back to life. The Ba was the head of the person with the body of a hawk. They also felt that a person's name and shadow lived on forever.

Sarcophagus: The sarcophagus is the case that the mummy rests inside while in the tomb. The inside and outside of the sarcophagus are elaborately decorated. The most famous sarcophagus is the gold and jeweled sarcophagus of King Tutankhamen.

GA1436

More Information About Ancient Egypt

King Tutankhamen: Tutankhamen was king from 1361 to 1352 B.C. He died at the age of 18. King Tut's tomb was discovered in 1922. Many good reference materials are available on King Tut and clearly show the magnificence of the King's tomb.

Pyramids: The Great Pyramids were burial temples for the great kings of Egypt. The pyramids were meant to represent stairways to the heavens. They were to protect the kings who were buried deep inside and provide space for the needed materials and wealth that would travel with them to the next world.

The Valley of the Kings: The building of the pyramids ended about 2150 B.C. By this time most of the pyramids had been robbed and the kings wanted to be buried in a place where the graves would not be found. The valley away from the Nile, deep in the desert, was considered the perfect location. Here in the cliffs and deep in the ground were buried many kings including Tutankhamen.

Crocodiles: There is a variety of crocodile known as the Nile crocodile. The largest known Nile crocodile grew to a length of 16 feet (4.8 m). Crocodiles are for the most part nocturnal. They prefer to bask in the sun during the day and do their hunting for food later in the evening. The most impressive part of a crocodile is its massive teeth. Crocodiles avoid areas with waves and strong wind. They prefer calm waters so they can rest with their nostrils slightly above the water's surface. Crocodiles lay clusters of eggs that can average from fifty to eighty eggs. Crocodiles will eat insects, frogs, snakes, fish and very large animals such as zebras, warthogs, cows and even people.

The Egyptian plover is a bird that is supposed to eat from the mouth of the Egyptian crocodile. The actual facts about this bird and its activity are hard to come by and some believe it to be a myth. The birds have been seen near crocodiles who are basking in the hot sun. When the crocodiles overheat they open their mouths to reduce their temperatures and the birds take advantage of the situation. In the extreme heat the crocodile would be rather docile and actually suffer from overheating.

GA1436

Oh What Big Teeth You Have!

If the Egyptian plover does act as a toothbrush to the crocodile by eating bits of food from his mouth, then this is a very courageous bird. Read the book *Dr. DeSoto* and write your own story about the brave toothbrush or the brave dentist.

_____

_____

_____

_____

_____

_____

_____

_____

_____

_____

_____

_____

_____

_____

_____

_____

GA1436

Graph Your Toothbrush Color

What color is your toothbrush? Color this toothbrush and cut it out.
Paste it on the class toothbrush graph.

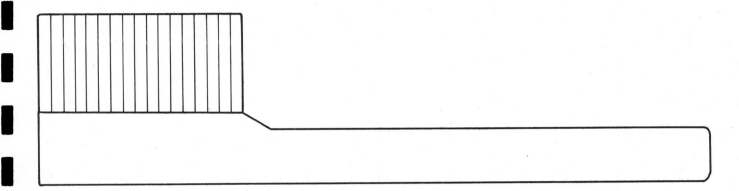

Once your class graph is done, color in your own graph. Remember to
start from the bottom when you color.

Number of Toothbrushes								
20								
18								
16								
14								
12								
10								
8								
6								
4								
2								
	red	orange	yellow	green	blue	purple		

GA1436

Baby Pictures

William Everett's baby picture was a picture of an egg on his bedroom wall. Draw baby pictures for these critters. Then write the name for them as babies.

A cat baby is called a _____.	A dog baby is called a _____.
A bird baby is called a _____.	A pig baby is called a _____.
You as a baby	A sheep baby is called a _____.

74

GA1436

That Great Long Name

In the story of *Bill and Pete,* William Everett Crocodile cried real crocodile tears because he couldn't spell his long name. According to the *Guinness Book of World Records* this is the world's longest name.

Rhoshandiatellyneshiaunneveshenk Koyaanfsquatsiuty Williams born to Mr. and Mrs. James Williams in Beaumont, Texas, on September 12, 1984.

Write a story about Rhoshan's first day of school when the teacher tried to teach her how to print her name.

_____

_____

_____

_____

_____

_____

_____

See if you can print Rhoshan's name and not forget any letters.

_____

_____

_____

_____

_____

_____

How many letters are in that great long name?_____

GA1436

What's in a Name?

William Everett Crocodile had a great long name, and he had trouble remembering all those letters until his friend Pete gave him a suggestion. Pete taught William how to shorten his name to Bill. Other names can be shortened. How do you shorten these names? Can you find the shortened names that will match?

Write in the shortened name for each.

Robert	Dave
Thomas	Jim
David	Sue
James	Bob
Susan	Dick
Frederick	Tom
Katherine	Joe
Richard	Fred
Joseph	Ray
Raymond	Katie
Charles	Mike
Kenneth	Don
Phillip	Larry
Michael	Ken
Donald	Charlie
Lawrence	Phil
Your name	Your nickname

GA1436

Design a cover for Bill's lunch box.

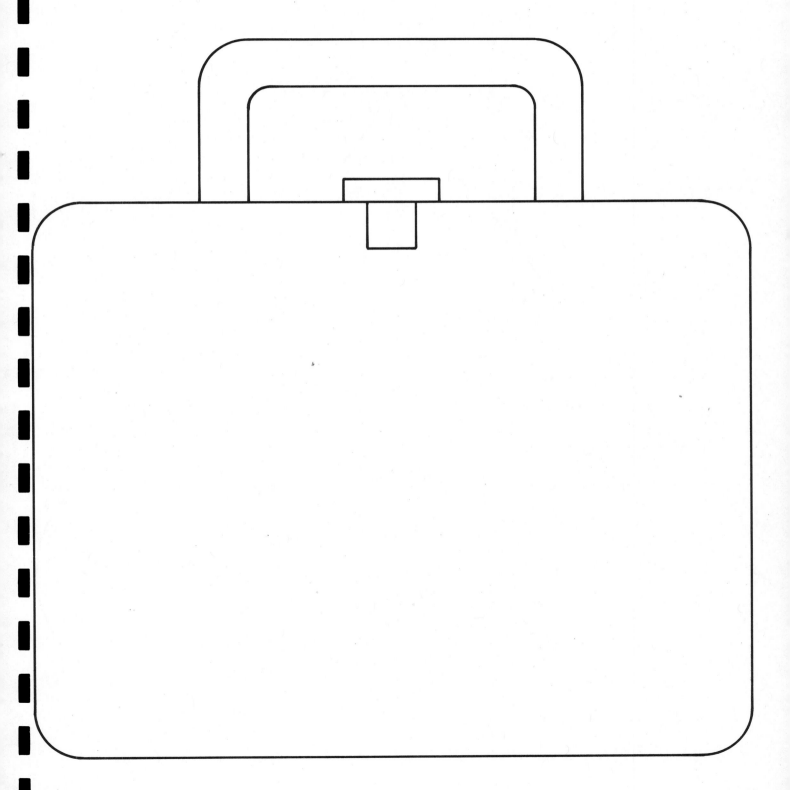

Big Old Crocodile Tears

Bill cried crocodile tears when he couldn't spell his name. What makes you cry?

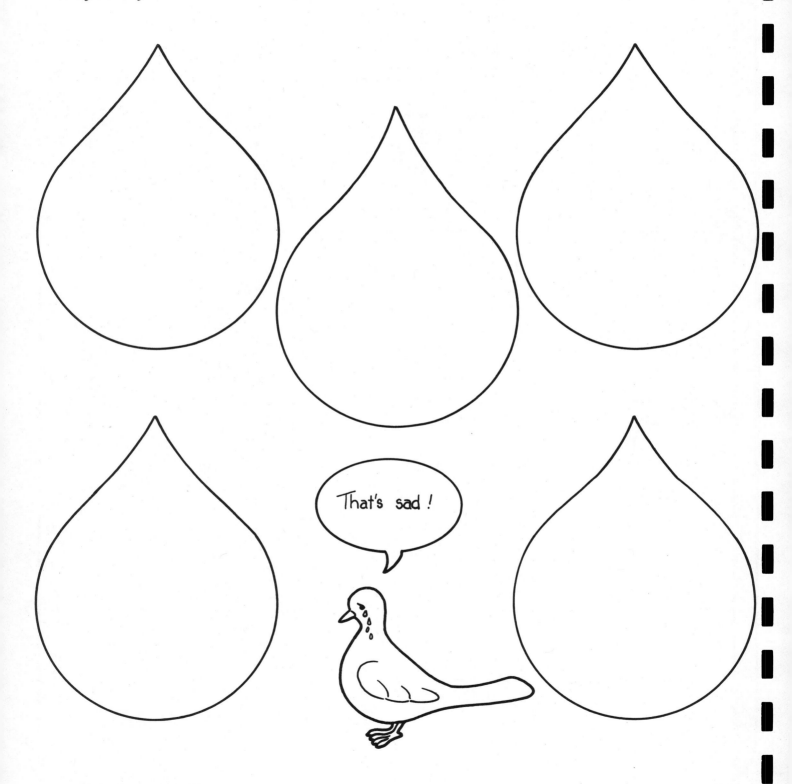

78

GA1436

Every student gets a report card. You get to be the teacher and give Bill his grades. Think carefully what grades you will give him and then make sure to write your comments on the report card so his mama will understand his report card.

Report Card
William Everett Crocodile

A–Wow!
B–Pretty Good
C–Just OK
D–Not So Hot
E–Oh Boy!

Being a good friend _____

Learning his ABC's _____

Being a good son _____

Learning to write his name _____

Staying away from strangers _____

Escaping _____

Teacher's Comments:

_____

_____

_____

_____

_____

_____

_____

_____

GA1436

Alligators of Ancient Egypt

In Ancient Egypt the Egyptians worshipped a powerful god that looked like a crocodile. Crocodiles were not considered scary but were raised in the temples and were treated like pets. The crocodiles were dressed in precious jewelry, and when they died they were made into mummies just like the kings.

Decorate the crocodile below and then list the problems that might occur when having a crocodile in the temple.

Problems with keeping a crocodile: _____

_____

_____

Advantages to keeping a crocodile: _____

_____

_____

"Charlie Needs a Cloak"

GA1436

"Charlie Needs a Cloak"

The theme of this book is product production. Any unit on product development can be enhanced by using this book. *"Charlie Needs a Cloak"* teaches about the production of wool with a great deal of humor and wit.

When teaching with this book, be sure to make available lots of different types of wool. Try to get the real objects or pictures of wool from the sheep, a carding brush, and a spinning wheel. The children would love to card the wool and feel the different types of textures of wool products.

The vocabulary in this book that may be new to children includes the following:

crook	sheared	dyed
flock	carded	strands
shepherd	spun	loom
cloak	pokeweed	wove

Since so many of the words in this book have consonant blends at the beginning, there is an activity page included that helps identify various consonant blend words.

The book also lends itself to an excellent lesson on sequence. None of the steps to making wool can be done out of order. The children can illustrate and briefly write about each of the steps, and the pages can be bound into a book.

The story also has a tiny substory told in pictures. A rebus story will help the children sequence the things that the little mouse takes from Charlie.

Of course the sheep has his own problems, and a writing activity encourages the children to tell the story through the eyes of the sheep.

This book is so rich with small details it will be fun for the children to read again and again. Don't forget to ask the children why they think the title *"Charlie Needs a Cloak"* is in quotes and who made the comment.

GA1436

"Charlie Needs a Cloak"

Make a Flock of Sheep

Materials:

clothespins: the type with springs, two for each sheep
tongue depressors, one for each sheep
cotton balls
jiggle eyes, two for each sheep
felt for ears

Procedure:

This activity is simple and cute when completed. The children attach
the clothespins to the tongue depressor creating a body and legs.

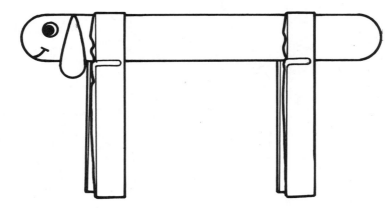

Next, the children attach the eyes to the tongue depressor. If you have
trouble making them stick, carefully use a hot glue gun or craft glue.

Finally, cover the entire body of the sheep with cotton balls. These
sheep stand by themselves and make a very nice flock along with Charlie and his crook.

GA1436

Consonant Blends

Color the words with consonant blends to discover the secret picture.

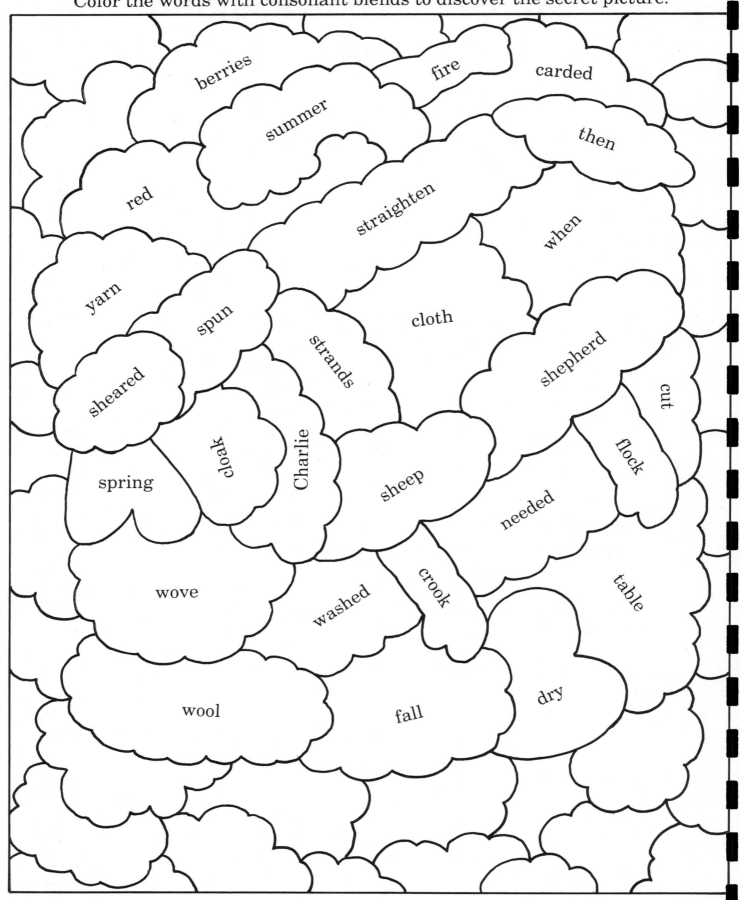

GA1436

The Sheep Tells His Story

Read *"Charlie Needs a Cloak"* and imagine you are the sheep. Look carefully at the illustrations. How does the sheep feel about Charlie before he gets sheared? How does he feel about the wool Charlie has taken from him? What does the sheep do when Charlie tries to turn the wool into cloth? What does the sheep do to Charlie's new coat?

Write the story as if it is being told by the sheep. Answer the questions above to help you remember all the parts of the story. Don't forget to write in complete sentences. Give the sheep a name and tell the story as if the sheep were telling what happened.

_____

_____

_____

_____

_____

_____

_____

_____

_____

_____

_____

_____

_____

_____

_____

GA1436

Follow That Mouse

In the story *"Charlie Needs a Cloak"* there is a tiny mouse that is telling his own story. Follow each page and write the story as if it is being told by the little mouse. Use the little pictures at the bottom of the page to help you tell the story. Cut out the pictures and glue them down when you tell what has happened. Use all the pictures.

"Charlie Needs a Cloak"
and
The Mouse Needs a Home

Once upon a time a little mouse was out in the field watching Charlie

shear his sheep. When Charlie wasn't looking, the little mouse took a

pair of   . When he saw Charlie washing the wool, the mouse

took the   ,   . Charlie was so busy carding the wool he didn't

notice the mouse taking the   . As Charlie spun the wool, the

little mouse decided to take some   for himself.

GA143

Charlie wanted his coat to be bright red but the little mouse had other

ideas for the _____. Charlie was so busy fighting with the sheep

by the loom he didn't notice the mouse as he took the _____. The

cloth was very beautiful, and the mouse enjoyed watching the sheep eat

the cloth while he quietly pulled away the _____. It was fall and

getting colder. Charlie began to cut the beautiful red cloth and the

mouse borrowed a _____. The mouse borrowed the

which Charlie needed when he pinned the cloth together. While Charlie

sewed, the mouse borrowed Charlie's _____. Then during the win-

ter the mouse found a warm _____. He spent a warm and cozy

winter in his new _____.

GA1436

How to make wool from the beginning . . .

to the end!

88

Shearing the Sheep

_____

_____

_____

_____

_____

Washing the Wool

_____

_____

_____

_____

_____

_____

GA1436

Carding the Wool

_____

_____

_____

_____

_____

Spinning the Wool

_____

_____

_____

_____

_____

GA143

The Wool Is Dyed

_____

_____

_____

_____

_____

The Yarn Is Woven

_____

_____

_____

_____

_____

The Cloth Is Cut

_____
_____
_____
_____
_____
_____

The Cloth Is Sewn

_____
_____
_____
_____
_____
_____

GA143

The Mysterious Giant of Barletta

GA1436

The Mysterious Giant of Barletta

The children will enjoy reading about the gentle giant of a statue that lives in the town of Barletta, Italy. The statue really does exist in the town and activities are included that acquaint the children with the country of Italy.

The statue is a mascot of sorts to the town much the same way the Statue of Liberty is a special symbol to Americans. Included in this unit you will find some special information about both statues and a place for the children to compare how they are alike and different.

Have the children create their own giant and have each team create a different part. Read to the children about the creation of the Statue of Liberty and see how each part of the statue was created and assembled.

Since Tomie de Paola likes to include Italian phrases in his books, a page has been included that allows the children to use context clues to discover the meanings of the words.

Encourage children to write about other adventures that happened after the soldiers left the city. What other things was the giant able to help the townspeople do? What kind of statue would the children design to protect their school or home? What would happen if each family on your street had a statue? What would the street look like and what kind of a statue would you want for your family?

GA143

You Know the Mystery

You have discovered the mystery of the giant of Barletta. You know why the statue was built and how it came to the square. Tell what it has in its hand and why he is pointing to the sky.

_____

_____

_____

_____

_____

_____

_____

Now that everyone knows the giant's story, it is time to give him a name.

_____

GA1436

A Day in the Life of a Statue

What's it like to be a statue? In your own mind pretend you are a statue in the middle of town. What would you see and do? How would you feel? What would be the best part of being a statue and what would be the worst part?

_____

_____

_____

_____

_____

_____

_____

Cut out the statue and paste it in the middle of a sentence strip. Fold your paper to make eight boxes and tell about a day in the life of your statue. Start early in the morning and go until late at night. Tell about everything your statue sees and feels.

GA143

The Real Town of Barletta

In Italy there is a town of Barletta with a real statue. Barletta is a coastal town along the Adriatic Sea. The statue is called *Colosso* which means "big" or "huge" in Italian. The statue stands alone and is 15 feet (4.56 m) high. It is said to be a statue of a long-ago Roman emperor named Valentinian I who lived from 364-375. The *Colosso* is made of bronze. In the years around 1300 some local people removed the arms and legs to make a bell from the body, but in 1941 the statue was restored. It has been there ever since.

Barletta

GA1436

Statue of Liberty

The Statue of Liberty is a famous female statue in the harbor of New York City. She is 151 feet (46.81 m) tall and when she stands on her pedestal and base, she is 154 feet (47.74 m) taller making her 305 feet (94.55 m) tall from top to bottom.

The Statue of Liberty was a gift to the United States from the country of France. Much of the money used to build the statue was collected from the school children of France. This money was only used to build the statue. The pedestal and base were built by the American people. The Statue of Liberty almost didn't come to America because the United States could not raise enough money to build the pedestal. Many people thought the statue was a silly idea and called it "Frenchman's Folly."

But when she finally arrived, everyone fell in love with the beautiful statue. Millions of people have seen the Statue of Liberty as they arrive in New York Harbor, and she has become a protective symbol of freedom.

GA1436

The Big Meeting

Imagine that the Statue of Liberty and the Mysterious Giant of Barletta meet. What do you think they would talk about? What adventures has each statue had? How do they feel about people and birds?

_____

_____

_____

_____

_____

_____

_____

Look at pictures and tell how the Statue of Liberty and the Mysterious Giant of Barletta are alike and different?

Alike	Different

GA1436

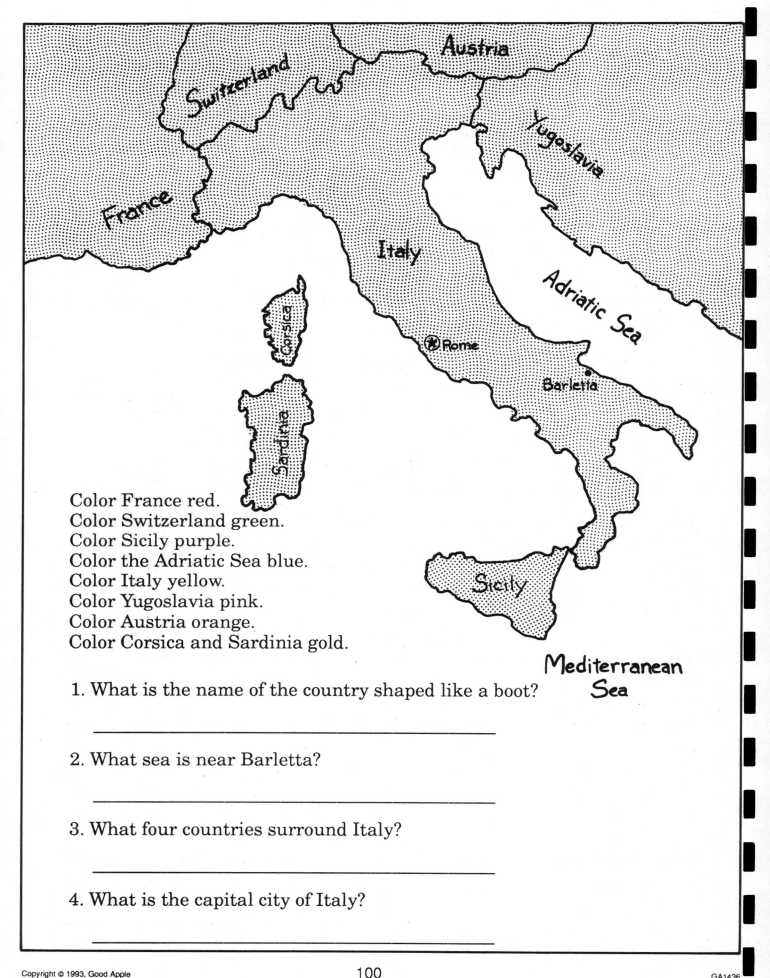

Color France red.
Color Switzerland green.
Color Sicily purple.
Color the Adriatic Sea blue.
Color Italy yellow.
Color Yugoslavia pink.
Color Austria orange.
Color Corsica and Sardinia gold.

1. What is the name of the country shaped like a boot?

_____

2. What sea is near Barletta?

_____

3. What four countries surround Italy?

_____

4. What is the capital city of Italy?

_____

The Giant's Tall Tale

In your own words, retell the story the Mysterious Giant told the soldiers.

_____

_____

_____

_____

_____

_____

_____

Retell a story you have told to save the day or get out of trouble.

_____

_____

_____

_____

_____

_____

_____

GA1436

Look! I Can Read Italian!

In the story Zia Concetta often speaks to the Mysterious Giant in Italian. Find where she or the giant are saying these words in the story and reread the sentence. See if you can figure out what she or the giant is saying.

Circle the answer you think is correct.

1. *buona notte* means

   be good   good night   watch out

2. *colosso* means

   bad boy   big one   don't forget

3. *buono fortuna* means

   good luck   smell this   hurry

4. *minuscolo* means

   very large   tiny   hungry

5. *debole* means

   silly   weakling   go away

6. *che bella festa* means

   at last   wonderful party   safe at last

7. *grazie* means

   thank you   hello   look out

Buona notte!

The townspeople have decided to put a plaque on the statue of the Mysterious Giant. This is what it says:

GA1436

Statue's Vacation

Being a statue is boring
I serve no purpose at all,
Except for the birds and the lovers
And the leaves that drop in the fall.

I can't ever go to a movie
Or swing on the swings at the park.
I never can eat at McDonald's;
I'm all alone after dark.

I'd like to ride on this horse;
He's tired of standing here too
To a place where statues vacation
On the island of Rockimandoo.

GA1436

Now One Foot,
Now the Other

GA1436

Now One Foot, Now the Other

This story looks at the close relationship between a boy and his grandfather. Much of the story revolves around the simple act of playing with blocks. Have your children use building blocks to build towers. Have them work in teams and see who can build the largest tower. After they have counted the blocks, graph the class results for each group.

Many schools now celebrate Grandparents' Day. The grandparents are invited to the school to see the children and participate in activities. If you do invite the grandparents to visit, ask them to share games they enjoyed playing as children and teach them to the children. We all learned how to play marbles after one visit by grandparents.

This unit provides teachers with the opportunity to discuss feelings of grief and dismay at the illness of a family member. It may help your children to have open-ended discussions about their feelings.

Have the children write about the perfect day they could spend with a grandparent. Ask them to tell and draw everything they would enjoy doing. The sky's the limit!

Don't forget to focus on the simple enjoyments that are present in this story. Many of the "special" things in Tomie de Paola's stories are simple things like making bread or sharing candy. Ask the children about simple things that they do with their families that make them happy. A focus in this direction is certainly needed by many children.

Another beautiful story of a grandfather and grandson is *Knots on a Counting Rope* by Bill Martin, Jr. The children might enjoy comparing these two stories of love between two generations.

GA1436

G Is for Grandfather

G is for Grandfather
He's daddy to my dad.
Grandma is my daddy's mom
And I'm their grandson Tad.

Read this poem carefully and draw a picture that shows all the people in the poem. After you have drawn the people, write who they are under the picture.

Now tell about your own grandpa and grandma. What do you like to do together?

_____

_____

_____

_____

GA1436

Now One Foot, Now the Other

1. Who was Bobby named after? _____

2. What was the first word Bobby said?_____

   Do you know what the first word you ever said was? _____

   If you know, what was the word? _____

   Did you know that most children learn to say their first word around their first birthday?

3. What would Bob say to Bobby as he taught him to walk?

   " _____ "

4. We all need other people to help us learn. What have you learned that your parents or grandparents helped you to do? Tell about what you learned and how you felt.

This Is What I Learned

_____

_____

_____

This Is Who Taught Me

_____

_____

_____

This Is How I Felt

_____

_____

_____

GA14

Sarah and Pop-Pop

"Did you know you're the best looking
  granddaughter I have?"
"I'm the only granddaughter you have!"

Silly grandpa—Silly girl

How's your belly button?
Pull my finger
Not my hair
There's not much there!

Let's play checkers.
Help me up.
I love you, Sarah
I love you, Pop-Pop.

GA1436

Last Block

Bob and Bobby Build a Tower

1. The third block has the letter *A* on the side.
2. The fifth block has a cat on the side.
3. The next to the last block has the number 9 on the side.
4. The first block has the letter *D* on the side.
5. The tenth block has a dog on the side.
6. The second block has the number 3 on the side.
7. The fourth block has a rooster on the side.
8. The eighth block has the letter *B* on the side.
9. The sixth block has a picture of a pig on the side.
10. The seventh block has the number 5 on the side.

How many blocks had numbers? _____

How many blocks had pictures? _____

How many blocks had letters?_____

First Block

GA1488

Losing a Friend

5. Write three sentences that tell how Bobby must have felt when he heard his grandfather had a stroke.

   a. _____

   b. _____

   c. _____

6. Pretend that you are Bobby. Write a page in his diary on the night Bobby heard the bad news about his best friend Bob.

Dear Diary,

   Dear Diary,

   _____

   _____

   _____

                                    Love, Bobby

7. What did Bobby's mother tell him was wrong with Bob? How was Bob different after the stroke?

   _____

   _____

   _____

GA1436

Bobby has written his grandfather a card in the hospital. Write a nice note and color a picture for grandfather.

But, you're the most special grandfather to me!

_____
_____
_____
_____
_____
_____
_____
_____
_____
_____

Grandfathers are special
As special as can be!

A Good Apple Card

GA1436

Bobby's Turn to Help

8. Bobby built a tower of blocks to cheer up his grandfather. What do you do to cheer up your parents or friends when they are sad?

_____

_____

_____

9. How did Bobby know that Bob would get better? _____

_____

10. Bobby had to do many things to help Bob get well. Tell what Bobby did to help his grandfather.

a. _____

_____

b. _____

_____

c. _____

_____

d. _____

_____

GA1436

Follow the Footsteps

After you read the story *Now One Foot, Now the Other,* cut out the footprints at the bottom and paste them on the footsteps in the order that they happened from first to sixth, keeping them in sequence. Each one tells about something that happened in the story.

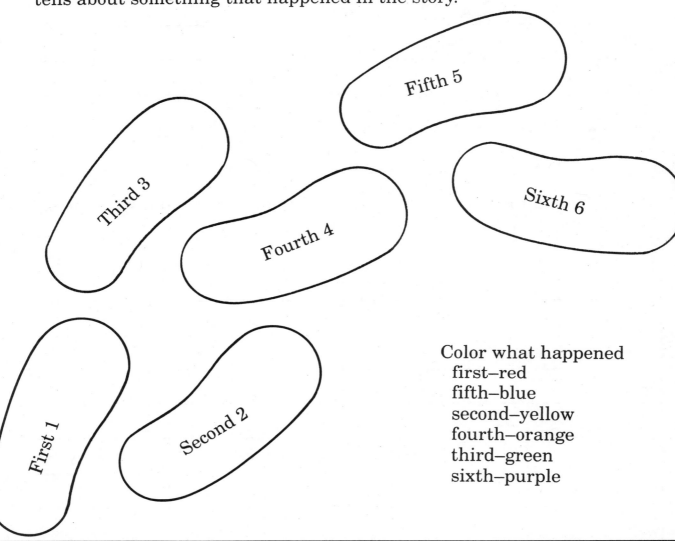

Fifth 5

Third 3

Sixth 6

Fourth 4

Color what happened
first–red
fifth–blue
second–yellow
fourth–orange
third–green
sixth–purple

First 1

Second 2

Bobby knew Bob would get better.

Bob got sick and went to the hospital.

Bobby was named after his grandpa.

Bobby was scared of his grandpa.

Bob and Bobby watched fireworks.

Bobby helped Bob walk again.

GA1436

Nana Upstairs
and
Nana Downstairs

Nana Upstairs and Nana Downstairs

This is a very sweet and touching story. The children may find the issue of death difficult, especially if someone in the class has recently experienced a death in the family.

The love between Tommy and his great-grandmother is one worth exploring with the children. Although she was very old and unable to do much, they still were able to share a joyful relationship.

In my classroom we did an entire unit on the elderly and the children gained a new respect for the older generation. We concluded our unit with a visit to a nursing home. The children and the elderly thoroughly enjoyed the visit. Here are some books that we also found helpful.

Kevin's Grandma by Barbara Williams
The Wednesday Surprise by Eve Bunting
Happy Birthday, Grampie by Susan Pearson
Wilfrid Gordon McDonald Partridge by Mem Fox

An activity is included where the children compare and contrast *Nana Upstairs and Nana Downstairs*. Discuss with the children the various abilities of each grandmother and the fact that the 94-year-old grandmother was once younger and more able to do for herself.

Use the idea of stars to make paper stars and discuss shooting stars. Take out the glitter and make a mess. Let the children make cards for their grandparents or elderly neighbors.

Finally, work to break the stereotypes of the elderly with the children. Older people can still ski, jump from planes and even tap dance. Just ask Tomie de Paola!

GA1436

Nana Upstairs and Nana Downstairs

1. How old was Tommy? _____

2. How old was Nana Upstairs? _____

3. How old was Nana Upstairs when Tommy was born? _____

4. Tell what a great-grandmother is? _____

   _____

   _____

5. What was Tommy's favorite toy? _____

6. Draw a picture of Tommy, Nana Downstairs, Nana Upstairs and his parents.

117

GA1436

How are Nana Upstairs and Nana Downstairs alike and different?

	Alike	**Different**
Where they live?		
How they look?		
What they do?		
Their hair?		
How they treated Tommy?		

Shooting Star

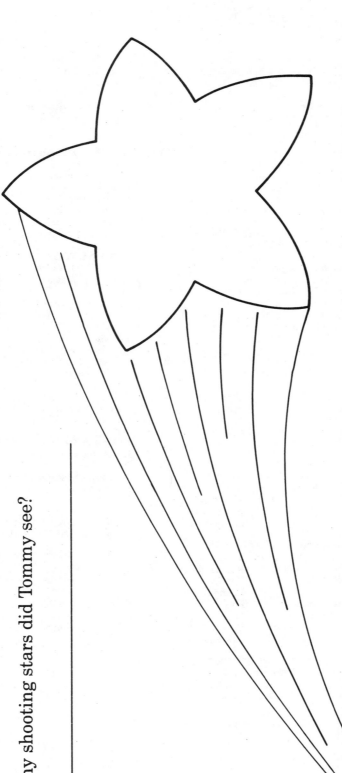

1. How many shooting stars did Tommy see?

_____

2. What happened when Tommy saw the second shooting star?

_____

3. How did this story make you feel? Explain.

_____

119

GA1436

Answer Key

STREGA NONA Pages 5-8
3. Franny and Fuffy
6. a word that tells action
7. a word that tells about a person, place or thing
8. pick the vegetables
   wash the dishes
   milk the goat
   sweep the house
   weed the garden
   fetch the water
9. a bed to sleep in and food to eat
10. thank you
11. yes

***Strega Nona* Crossword Puzzle** Page 14

Across
1. Strega Nona
3. Big Anthony
5. si
6. pasta pot
7. bubbling

Down
2. grazie
4. kisses
8. Calabria
9. magic
10. eat

THE POPCORN BOOK Page 19
Boys' names—Tiny and Tony

Popcorn Facts Page 20
1. 4600 years
2. 5600 years
3. Indians selling popcorn jewelry
4. South America; answers will vary
5. popped it
6. There are mountains and llamas.
7. field corn, feed corn, popcorn
8. 1000 years

500,000,000 Pounds of Popcorn Page 25
Movies, etc., 30%
Seed, etc., 10%
Home, 60%

Facts and Opinions About Popcorn Page 26
1. fact
2. opinion
3. opinion
4. fact
5. opinion
6. fact
7. opinion
8. opinion
9. fact
10. opinion

MICHAEL BIRD-BOY
Mix and Match Page 34
1. genuine—not artificial or fake
2. shoo—yell to chase away
3. fly—a small insect
4. artificial—made by man, not nature
5. honey—made by bees, sweet
6. syrup—a thick, sweet, sticky liquid
7. opposite—genuine, artificial

FIN M'COUL Pages 45-46
1. Fin M'Coul—Oonagh
3. kin: family
   causeway: road
4. The earth trembled and he flattened a thunderbolt.
5. He had beaten all the rest
6. a. brought him slippers
   b. lit his pipe
   c. stirred the peat fire
   d. gave him a mug of stout
   e. cut him a slab of soda bread

7. a. one on her right arm
   b. one around her right ankle
   c. one circling her heart

Could So! Could Not! Page 47
1. could so—people can braid
2. could so—you could bake something inside the bread
3. could not—too big
4. could not—fantasy
5. could not—stones wouldn't look or feel like cheese
6. could so
Answers may vary with discussion.

THE KNIGHT AND THE DRAGON
Be the Castle Librarian Page 58
A Guide to Dragons
Catch a Dragon
Dragon Delight
Everyday Guide to Fighting
Fight a Dragon
How to Fight a Dragon
Knights and Dragons
Making Armor

Secret, Silent Words of the Knight and the Dragon Page 61
Knight
fight
rough
tough
caught
knight

fought
through
castle
fighting
toughest

BILL AND PETE and BILL AND PETE GO DOWN THE NILE
Baby Pictures Page 74
cat—kitten
bird—chick

dog—puppy
pig—piglet
sheep—lamb

What's in a Name? Page 76
Robert—Bob
Thomas—Tom
David—Dave
James—Jim
Susan—Sue
Frederick—Fred
Katherine—Katie
Richard—Dick

Joseph—Joe
Raymond—Ray
Charles—Charlie
Kenneth—Ken
Phillip—Phil
Michael—Mike
Donald—Don
Lawrence—Larry

"CHARLIE NEEDS A CLOAK"
Consonant Blends Page 84
shepherd
crook
flock
sheep
Charlie
cloak
spring

sheared
spun
strands
cloth
when
then
straighten

The Mouse Needs a Hom Pages 86-87
1. scissors
2. soap
3. apple
4. yarn
5. berries
6. candle
7. cup
8. jack-o'-lantern
9. ruler
10. boot
11. mitten
12. house

THE MYSTERIOUS GIANT OF BARLETTA Page 100
1. Italy
2. Adriatic Sea
3. France, Switzerland, Austria, Yugoslavia
4. Rome

Look! I Can Read Italian! Page 102
1. buona notte—good night
2. colosso—big one
3. buono fortuna—good luck
4. minuscolo—tiny
5. debole—weakling
6. che bella festa—wonderful party
7. grazie—thank you

NOW ONE FOOT, NOW THE OTHER
Pages 108, 111 and 113
1. his grandfather
2. Bob
3. Now one foot, now the other.
7. He sat in a chair and didn't talk or move.
9. Bob sneezed at the elephant block.
10. a. He helped feed him.
    b. Bobby sat outside with him.
    c. Bobby told him stories.
    d. He helped him walk.

Follow the Footsteps Page 114
1. Bobby was named after his grandpa.
2. Bob and Bobby watched fireworks.
3. Bob got sick and went to the hospital.
4. Bobby was scared of his grandpa.
5. Bobby knew Bob would get better.
6. Bobby helped Bob walk again.

NANA UPSTAIRS AND NANA DOWNSTAIRS Page 117
1. 4
2. 94
3. 90
5. Bunny

Shooting Star Page 119
1. two
2. His Nana Downstairs died.

GA1436

Bulletin Board Ideas

Using bulletin board extensions is a good way to build language skills into a literature-based classroom. Many of the ideas can be altered to accommodate any of the skill areas. Children learn more by having opportunities to create the bulletin board, and they also enjoy using the bulletin board as a learning center when possible.

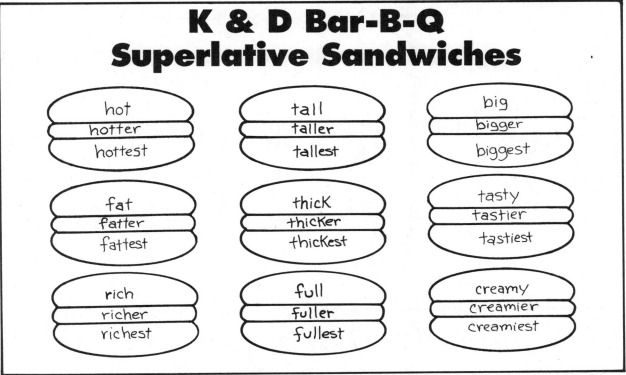

K & D Bar-B-Q Superlative Sandwiches

hot
hotter
hottest

tall
taller
tallest

big
bigger
biggest

fat
fatter
fattest

thick
thicker
thickest

tasty
tastier
tastiest

rich
richer
richest

full
fuller
fullest

creamy
creamier
creamiest

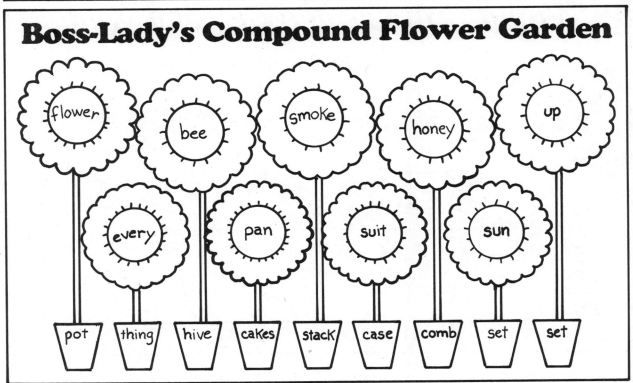

Boss-Lady's Compound Flower Garden

flower

bee

smoke

honey

up

every

pan

suit

sun

pot | thing | hive | cakes | stack | case | comb | set | set

GA1436

Corn Is Poppin' at the Circus

Hard "C"   Soft "C"

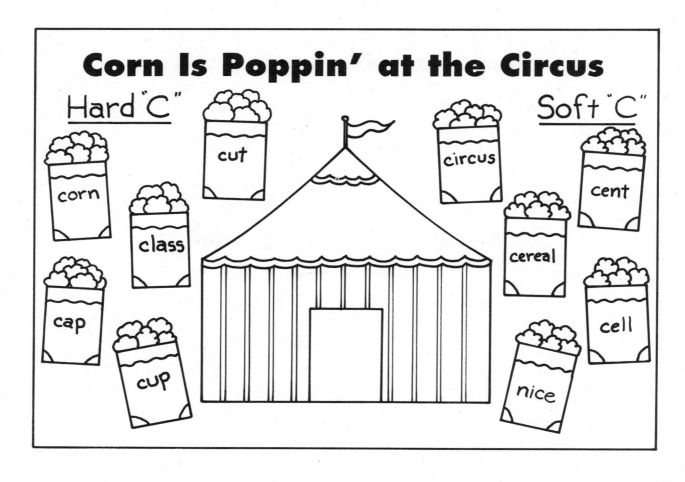

cut

corn

class

cap

cup

circus

cent

cereal

cell

nice

What Other Things from A to Z Would Scare Away the Bad Guy?

A H I L M P Q T

B J K O R S U

Bat

C G N V

W

F

D E X Y

Dog Z

GA1436

Building Block Contractions
for Bob and Bobby

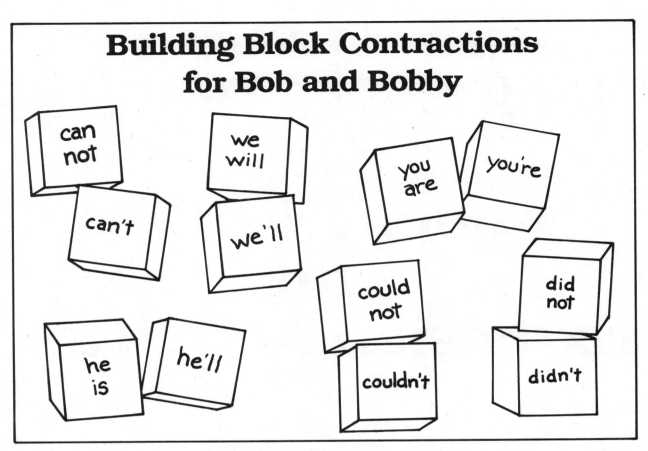

(Other contractions you can include are he'll, doesn't, don't, wasn't.)

Fin M'Coul Fairies Love Homophones

(Other words you can include are beat-beet, male-mail, week-weak, feet-feat, tail-tale.)

GA1436

Book Cover Designs
for
Student Writing
and
Extension Activities

Making Books for Student Writing and Extension Activities

The following pages include formats for having your children make individual and class books. In our school we have a machine that spiral binds the books. Each of the illustrations has one side that has a straight edge if you choose to spiral bind. The books can also be stapled together.

The pictures can be enlarged for class books which allow participation by each child in the classroom. Many of the extension activities that were suggested in each book chapter can also be completed in these books.

You can also use these shapes for bulletin boards and classroom extension activities.

GA1436

The Art Lesson

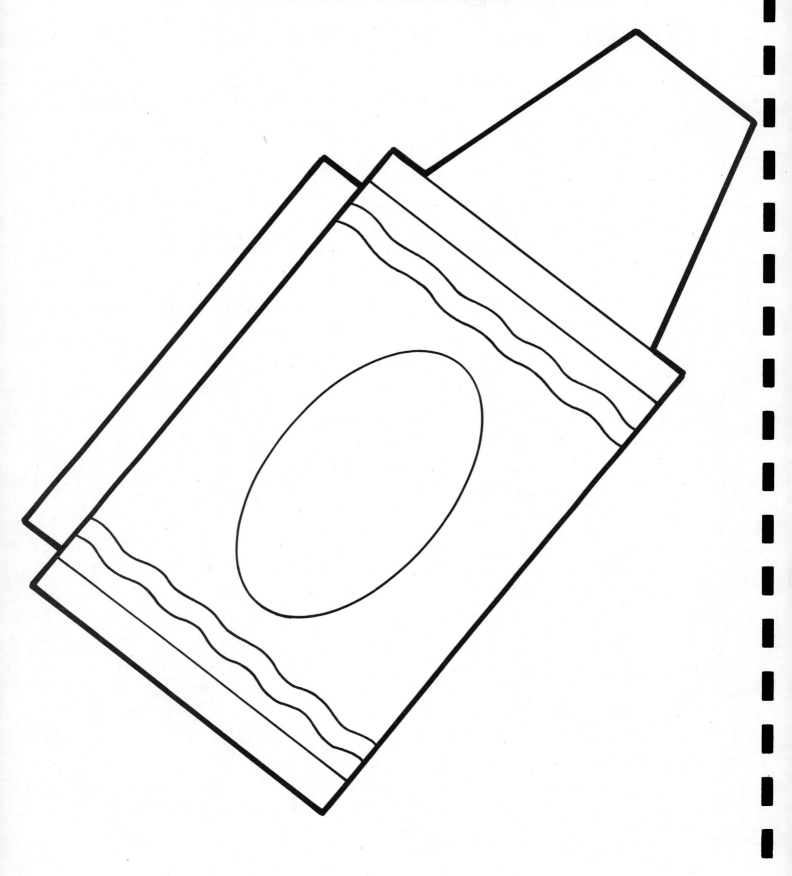

126

Strega Nona

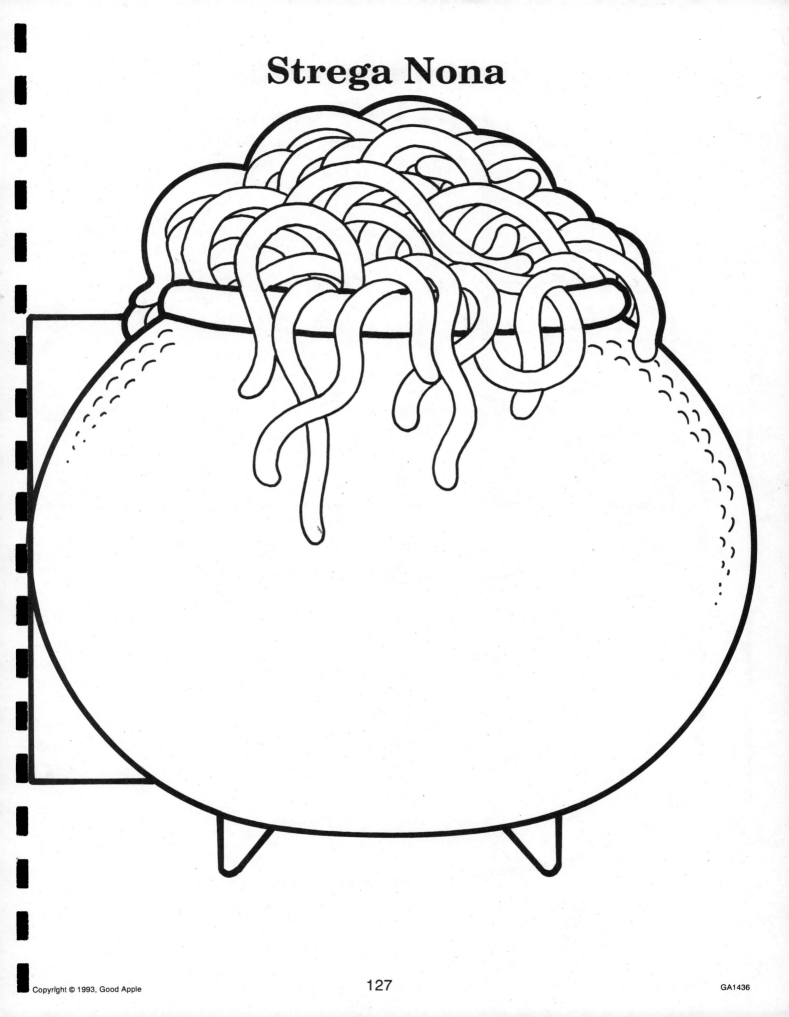

The Popcorn Book

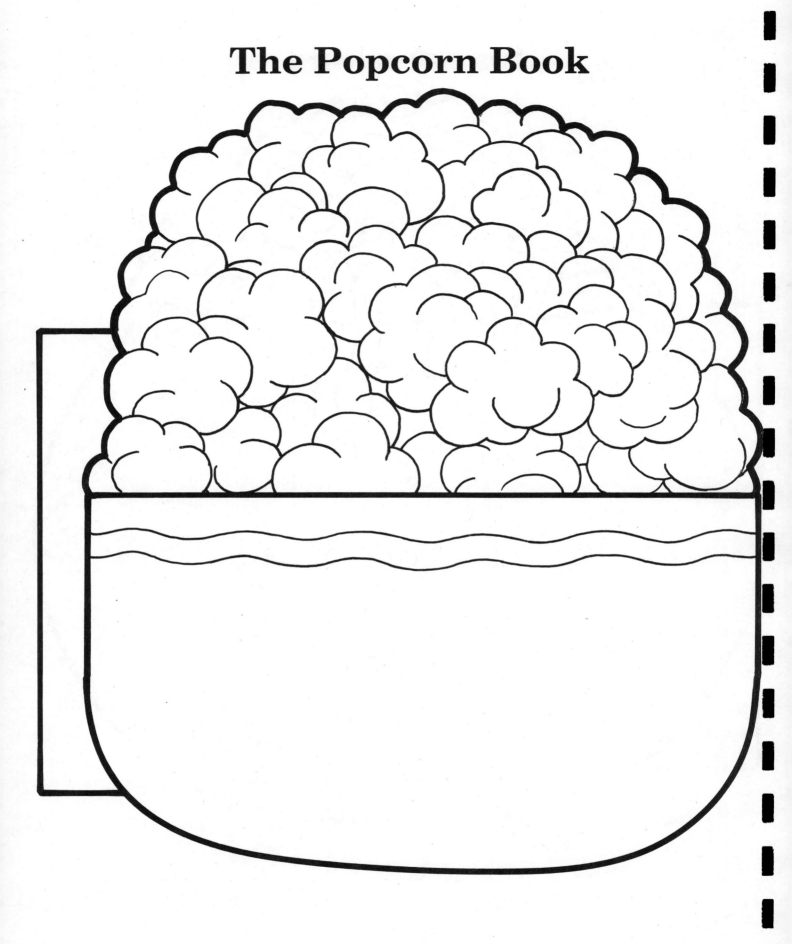

128

GA1436

Michael Bird-Boy

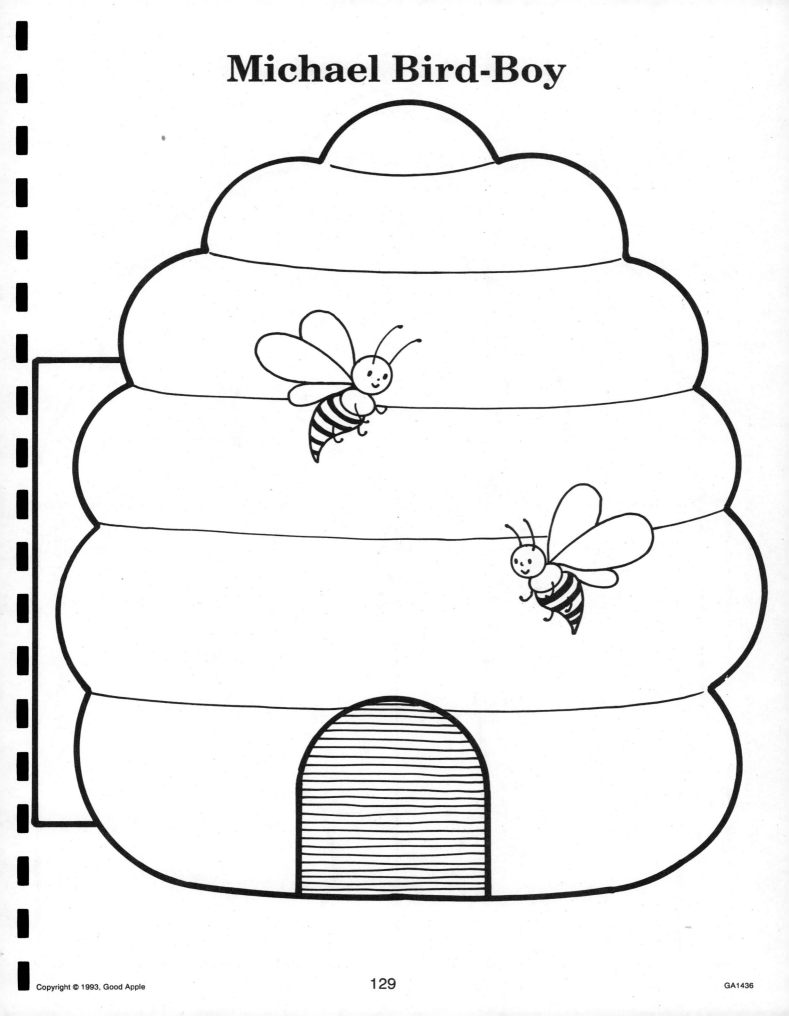

GA1436

Fin M'Coul

130

The Knight and the Dragon

GA1436

Watch Out for the Chicken Feet in Your Soup

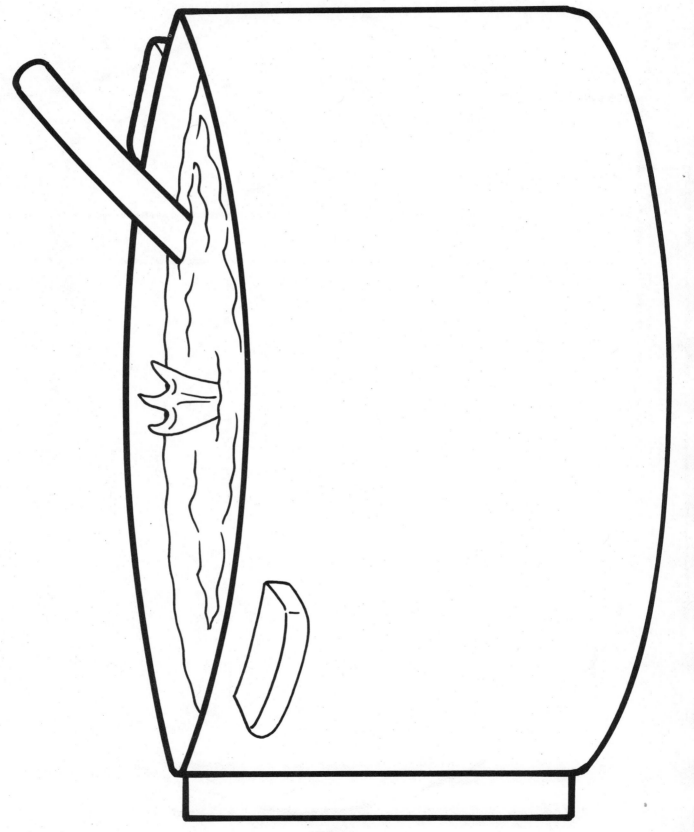

Bill and Pete

133

GA1436

Bill and Pete Go down the Nile

134

"Charlie Needs a Cloak"

135

The Mysterious Giant of Barletta

136

GA1436

Now One Foot, Now the Other

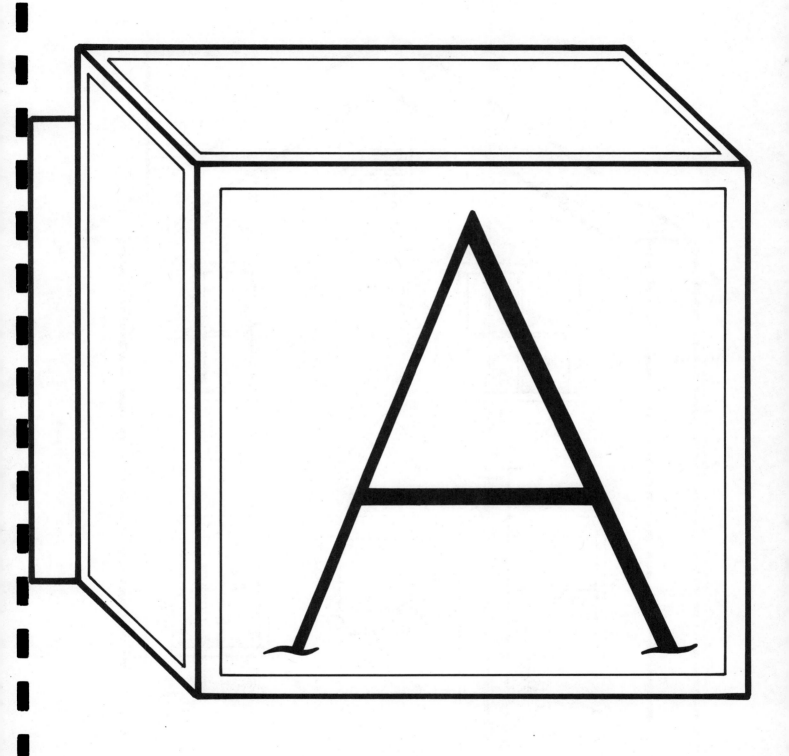

137

Nana Upstairs and
Nana Downstairs

GA1436